0012590

Prentice-Hall, Inc., Englewood Cliffs, New Jersey 07632

Roy R. Behrens

University of Wisconsin—Milwaukee

Design
in the
Visual Arts

Library of Congress Cataloging in Publication Data

BEHRENS, ROY R., 1946–
    Design in the visual arts.

    Bibliography: p.
    Includes index.
    1. Design. I. Title.
NK1510.B475 1984   745.4   83-3274
ISBN 0-13-201947-7

Editorial/production supervision: Patricia V. Amoroso
Interior and cover design: Judith A. Matz
Page layout: Charles H. Pelletreau
Manufacturing buyer: Harry P. Baisley

Cover illustration: Warren Taylor. *Plum Funny.* 1980. Watercolor, 16″ × 28″. Courtesy the artist. This exquisitely humorous work is indeed "plum funny." It is a Sunday brunch of hue and tone that makes the mind's eye giggle because of its color surprises. Notice the skillful arrangement of the richly colored plums, which both support and contradict the strict perspective avenues which border the funny page panels. It would be a lesser work if the shadows of the plums were not diagonally poised.

The untitled four-line poem by Ezra Pound, quoted in Chapter 5, is reprinted by permission of New Directions Publishing Corporation and Faber and Faber Ltd. The poem appears in the books *Personnae*, copyright © 1926 by Ezra Pound, and *Collected Shorter Poems* by Ezra Pound.

The poem "Truth" by James Hearst, quoted in Chapter 5, is from James Hearst, *Limited View*, Iowa City, Iowa: Prairie Press, 1962. Copyright 1962 by James Hearst. Reprinted by permission of the author.

The following illustrations were originally published as covers or short story illustrations in various issues of *The North American Review:* Figures 2-3, 2-11, 3-2, 3-4, 3-15, 3-16, 4-10, and 5-2.

I am grateful to Robley Wilson, Jr., *The North American Review*, and the University of Northern Iowa for permission to use brief passages and several illustrations from my book, *Art and Camouflage: Concealment and Deception in Nature, Art and War.* Cedar Falls, Iowa: The North American Review, 1981.

Dedicated to Arthur Koestler

Printed in the United States of America

10 9 8 7 6 5 4 3 2 1

ISBN 0-13-201947-7

PRENTICE-HALL INTERNATIONAL, INC., *London*
PRENTICE-HALL OF AUSTRALIA PTY. LIMITED, *Sydney*
EDITORA PRENTICE-HALL DO BRASIL, LTDA., *Rio de Janiero*
PRENTICE-HALL CANADA INC., *Toronto*
PRENTICE-HALL OF INDIA PRIVATE LIMITED, *New Delhi*
PRENTICE-HALL OF JAPAN, INC., *Tokyo*
PRENTICE-HALL OF SOUTHEAST ASIA PTE. LTD., *Singapore*
WHITEHALL BOOKS LIMITED, *Wellington, New Zealand*

Contents

Preface and Acknowledgments

This book has resulted from the simple yet perplexing fact that much of my pain and pleasure in life derive from my role as a teacher. I would like to be an excellent teacher, especially an excellent teacher of art, since that is what I love and know. As do all who like to teach, I have searched for and mused about what I ought to teach in class and how I ought to teach it.

Throughout the years I've taught design, I have felt the sorry lack of a *clear* and yet *inventive* source on visual esthetic design. There are excellent books in print. There are publications which deal with composition, the elements and principles of design, color notation systems, and perceptual traits of art. Yet virtually none of them talks about where these notions came from, why they are to be believed, or how they relate to life.

Similarly, there are innumerable volumes on creativity, metaphor, and problem-solving, yet almost none of those books deals at length with visual art.

It has always seemed to me that a book on visual esthetic design could not be of lasting worth unless it addressed both these realms—*design* and *creativity*—within the complex context of everyday thinking and seeing. Whatever its imperfections and flaws, this book attempts to do just that.

The book consists of two main parts. The *history and theory* of design and creativity are presented in Chapters 1 through 5. The *process* of designing and sample *problems* are offered in the second part. Both parts have resulted from actual classroom struggles, from my classroom lectures and from problems I have used.

As do most books of this sort, I might have reproduced those familiar artworks that teachers and students have come to expect in any volume on design—Grant Wood's *American*

Gothic, a taste of Leonardo, two Picassos, a Seurat, and a Mondrian. I have chosen not to. It seemed to me a fresher way to use unknown examples—works by gifted artists, rarely shown in any books, and by students I have taught, who constantly amaze me.

This book is useful, I would think, for courses in foundations in both two-dimensional and three-dimensional visual esthetic design. Insofar as I can tell, distinctions of dimension and medium are not quintessential to what defines a thing as "art," and as the Appendix explains, I would have no qualms about using the two-dimensional problems in this book (slightly modified of course) as three-dimensional problems, or indeed, vice versa. There is no *essential* breach between two-dimensional and three-dimensional design. The basic prescripts are the same.

My teachers taught me how to teach. They also taught me how to write. My students make me *want* to teach. I am grateful to my colleagues, friends, and students at the University of Wisconsin—Milwaukee.

I am especially grateful to Charles Vansen, one of the finest teachers I know, whose friendship and exchanges have been essential to this book; to E. Tom Geniusz, whose loyalty, humor, and camera skills have resulted in excellent photographs of the students' works; to Susan Miles, a superb fellow artist, who offered generous assistance throughout the preparation of the book; to Robley Wilson, Jr., an excellent writer of fiction, friend, and editor of *The North American Review,* in which some of my students have been able to publish their works; to Guy Davenport, one of the most gifted writers of our time, who has tolerated the interruption of our four-year correspondence; to Michael P. Tomaro, for support and friendship in my moments of self-doubt; and to Mary Snyder Behrens, the paramount person in my life and the most remarkable person I know.

Finally and foremost, these words would not be on this page except for the tolerant foresight of Norwell Therien, Jr., my editor at Prentice-Hall. I am indebted to him, to his assistant, Jean Wachter, to my production editor, Patricia Amoroso, and to the staff at Prentice-Hall, without whose trust and expertise this book would not now be in print.

Roy R. Behrens

Associate Professor of Art
Department of Art
University of Wisconsin—Milwaukee
Milwaukee, Wisconsin 53201

Part One

History and Theory

Chapter 1

Esthetics and Anesthetics

What Is Design?

Design is organization. When anything is designed, it is "put together" with some intent or goal in mind. Everything that is not entirely accidental is, to some extent, designed.

Music is designed. Coffee is designed. Marriages are designed. So are books about design, pocket calculators, jokes, bank robberies, and firecrackers. Some designs are utterly simple; some astoundingly complex. Some succeed; others fail. Whenever something is purposely done, someone has *designed* it.

Some things are designed in a highly deliberate fashion. Some are designed in a casual way. But each can be constructed with some intent or goal in mind. Further, intentions are not always conscious, as Freud and other psychoanalysts have stressed. Less than conscious kinds of design include dreams, slips of the tongue, and psychopathological acts.

Things are almost always designed with more than one purpose in mind. Most firecrackers, for example, are not only designed to explode; they are also designed with safety in mind. In much the same way, I have rarely had a meal that

DESIGN Anything that is arranged, constructed, or organized with some intent or goal in mind. Anything that is purposely done can be said to be designed.

3

FIGURE 1-1 Chris Van Allsburg. *The Disappearing Egg Cup.* 1980. Conte on paper, 30″ × 40″. Courtesy the artist and Allan Stone Gallery, New York. Repeated features in this work include the folds of cloth, eggs, checkered squares, and egg cups. The strict symmetry is offset by the light source from the left, the precise placement of the three eggs on the table, the disruptive shadows, and the increasing transparency of the egg cups.

FIGURE 1-2 Douglas Sunquist. *Untitled.* 1982. Gouache, *8″ × 12″.* Courtesy the artist (student, University of Wisconsin—Milwaukee). The two dancing figures imply a bilateral symmetry which is dramatically broken by the glass and wedge shape on the left. This work was an answer to two-dimensional Problem Two, described in Chapter 6.

was designed only to be nutritious. Dinners are often also designed to be good-tasting, pleasing to the eye, reasonably priced, exotic, surprising, and so on.

When people argue about the quality of things, they are usually arguing about which design intentions should be most important. For example, when two people argue about the quality of a fast-food hamburger, one person may say that it's "horrible" because it lacks nutrition, whereas the other might say it's "superb" because it's cheap and quick to eat. Evaluations of anything are always made in terms of one or more intentions, which may be clear or hidden.

Arguments about the quality of works of art are a lot like arguments about the quality of fast-food hamburgers. An investment broker may say that an artwork is "bad" because if its market value falls, it was a poor investment. An historian may claim that the very same work is "good" because it clearly documents the customs of a time or place. A psychologist may tell us that the same work is invaluable because it clearly demonstrates the workings of the human mind. A technician might call that same work terrible because it is lacking in craftsmanship. These people need not argue. Each of their statements could be right. They are looking at the same thing in terms of vastly different values.

Visual Esthetic Design

A book about cooking would talk about culinary design. In a book about fire-crackers, I would discuss the design of explosives. As it happens, this book concerns design in art. More specifically, it is an introduction to what is called *visual esthetic design,* which occurs most often (not always) within works of visual art. To be sure, it is found elsewhere also—in meals that are pleasing to look at, in attractive clothing, in designs of chairs, and so on.

When I say *visual* esthetic design, I mean those kinds of objects which are (whatever else they do) primarily meant to be looked at. In the same way, musical compositions (however else they might be used) are primarily made to be listened to, and cooking is addressed to taste. This does not imply that works of visual art must be made *only* for the eye. Along with their visual features, they might also be designed to be tasted, touched, listened to, smelled, flown in the air, or thought about. However, it does imply that in works of this sort, visual organization is of central importance.

There are sincere and intelligent artists who would argue that visual organization is not of primary importance. Some, those who make *conceptual art,* would say that the primary purpose of art is to convey ideas (concepts), regard-

I learned from her and others like her that a first-rate soup is more creative than a second-rate painting. . . . From a young athlete, I learned that a perfect tackle could be as esthetic a product as a sonnet and could be approached in the same creative spirit.

Abraham Maslow, *Toward a Psychology of Being* (Princeton, N.J.: Van Nostrand, 1968).

I think it likely that there are no finer galleries of abstract art than the cabinet drawers of the tropical butterfly collector. . . .

Sir Alister Hardy, *The Living Stream* (New York: Harper and Row, 1965), p. 151.

VISUAL DESIGN Anything that is primarily made to be seen, in the same sense that music is usually made to be heard. Obviously, other senses and sensibilities can be addressed at the same time.

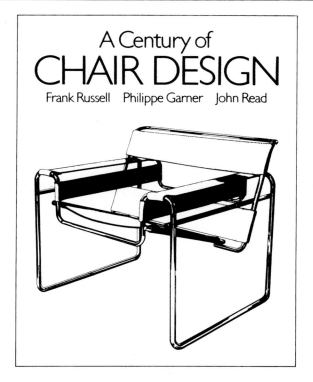

FIGURE 1-3   Frank Russell. Book jacket design for *A Century of Chair Design* by F. Russell, P. Garner, and J. Read (New York: Rizzoli International Publishers, 1980; and London: Academy Editions, 1980). Featured on the cover is Marcel Breuer's deservedly famous tubular steel chair, designed at the Bauhaus in 1925. Breuer was remarkably successful in designing furniture which was both esthetic and highly functional.

less of their visual form. Purposely, these artists may make little or no attempt to organize the appearance of their works. Others, those who make *performance art,* would say that the primary goal of art is to involve the audience in the work by making some event occur. These artists' views are not necessarily wrong, but unless they organize the appearance of their works (and some conceptual and performance artists certainly do), their intentions are different from those of visual esthetic design.

Unity with Variety

When I say visual *esthetic* design, I am talking about a certain kind of visual organization which, at least since ancient Greece, has been most often referred to as *unity with variety.*

I feel a recipe is only a theme, which an intelligent cook can play each time with a variation.

Madame Benoit.

ESTHETIC DESIGN Anything characterized by an approximate mixture of unity with variety. Any kind of construction, in any material, can possess this characteristic, since a design need not be visual (nor does it have to be art) to be called esthetic. Encounters with esthetically designed objects can be pleasant or unpleasant, enthralling or disturbing, but in general they exhort a heightening of our ability to perceive the kind, location, and timing of things.

VISUAL ESTHETIC DESIGN Constructions or arrangements which are primarily addressed to the eye and which are characterized by the structural feature of unity with variety. A design can be visual without being esthetic, or it can be esthetic without being visual.

. . . at moments of intense aesthetic experience we see not only with our eyes but with our whole body. The eyes scan, the cortex thinks, there are muscular stresses, innervations of the organs of touch, sensations of weight and temperature, visceral associations, feelings of rhythm and motion— all sucked into one vortex. . . .

Arthur Koestler, *The Act of Creation* (New York: Macmillan, 1964).

Obviously, one can make esthetic forms which are not addressed to sight. Thus, composers talk about "theme and variation" in musical compositions, poets use repeated sounds (rhyme and alliteration), and dancers make recurring moves. Forms which are esthetic are most often found in the arts. In fact, there are those who would insist that if a thing does not possess a high degree of unity with variety, it should not even be called "art," just as there are those who say that if a hamburger is not nutritious, it should not be labeled "food."

In addition, esthetic patterns are frequently found in things which one would not call art. There are natural forms which are characterized by unity with variety, as well as "nonart" functional forms.

You should be aware that there are all sorts of people who claim to be practicing artists who do not understand this concept of visual esthetic design. Further, there are artists who fully understand this concept but who do not believe in it. Finally, there are thousands of artworks in museums and galleries throughout the world which are poor examples of visual esthetic design. It is common and perfectly normal for museums and galleries to collect and exhibit things with design intentions that are not esthetic. Some intentions may be technical, economic, narrative, psychological, anthropological, historical, innovative, or therapeutic. This does not mean that these things are "bad," except in terms of esthetics.

Esthetics and Anesthetics

Esthetic is the opposite of *anesthetic*. When a person is given an anesthetic, a state of unconsciousness or insensitivity is artificially induced. Esthetics, on the other hand, involves the enhancement of feeling.

In a state of anesthesia, we can no longer determine the kind, location, and timing of things. Our sense of the order of things is numbed. In contrast, a state of esthetic perception increases our awareness and sharpens our sensitivity. When things are esthetically organized, we get a firmer grasp of the kind, location, and timing of things.

Obviously, anesthesia is not necessarily a "bad" state—in fact, it's a highly desirable state if one is undergoing major surgery. It is also a "good" state in terms of certain religious ideals, commonly found throughout the world, in which a person wants to be oblivious to (to be unaware of) the physical reality of daily life in the hope of attaining a higher state.

FIGURE 1-4 The pictorial content of the works of Francis Bacon is disturbing and repellent. However, when viewed as esthetic arrangements, his paintings are exquisite examples of unity with variety. In *Self-Portrait* (1970), on which this diagram is based, there is a rhythmic recurrence of oval shapes (indicated by arrows).

Anesthesia of this kind can be induced without a drug. It can be brought about by sustained exposure to extreme *repetition* (chanting) or extreme *variation* (frenzied dancing and shouting). The first of these states (with which you are familiar in the form of hypnosis) is called a *meditative trance*, which is characterized by peaceful inactivity in which one may not move for days. The second is called an *ecstatic trance*, which is characterized by seemingly fitful behavior, for example, speaking in tongues (*glossolalia*), or sudden trembling seizures.

As different as these two states are (one very passive; the other hysterical), they are referred to as *trances* because both result in an insensitivity to the things and events of daily life. It is generally believed that anesthetics of this sort can be so effective that persons within trances can radically alter their respiration and heartbeat, walk on piles of red-hot coals, lie on beds of nails, and so on.

By now, it may have occurred to you why these two states are anesthetic. The meditative state is unity *without* variety. It is extreme similarity, monotony, repetition. The ecstatic state is variety *without* unity. It is extreme difference,

ANESTHETIC DESIGN Constructions or arrangements characterized by unity *without* variety (extreme repetition) or variety *without* unity (extreme variation). Prolonged encounters with anesthetic phenomena can result in a numbing of the senses, much as in drug-induced anesthesia, in which we can no longer perceive the kind, location, and timing of things.

Therefore if you desire to discover your soul, withdraw your thoughts from outward and material things, forgetting, if possible, your own body and its five senses.
Walter Hilton.

ABCDEFGHI
JKLMNOPQ
RSTUVWXY
Zabcdefghij
klmnopqrst
uvwxyz 123
4567890&?
!£$ß()⅞⁒⸙

FIGURE 1-5 Styles of type, like works of art, are characterized by a mixture of similarities and differences. All letters in a typeface must be sufficiently similar so that they appear to belong together as examples of that font. At the same time, each letter must be sufficiently distinct from other letters so that they will not be confused.

. . . [in camouflage] we have a system of coloration the exact opposite of that upon which an artist depends when painting a picture. . . . The one makes something unreal recognizable: the other makes something real unrecognizable.

Hugh B. Cott, "Camouflage in Nature and in War," in *The Royal Engineers Journal,* December 1938, p. 506.

chaos, variation. Esthetic forms, as we have said, are characterized by unity *with* variety, by similarity with difference, by repetition with variation.

Order and Disorder

Order, as Rudolf Arnheim has said, "makes it possible to focus on what is alike and what is different, what belongs together and what is segregated." Anesthetically organized forms are types of perceptual *disorder,* in the sense that they prevent us from making distinctions of kind, location, and timing. They prevent us from focusing on what is similar and what is different.

When there is unity without variety (monotony), all things are the same. When there is variety without unity (chaos), everything is so different that no two parts can make a thing. These two principles are the essential ingredients of military camouflage, which is a perfect example of intentional anesthetic design.

Camouflage, like states of trance, is a form of disorder, because it is intended to prevent us from making distinctions of kind, location, and timing. In World Wars I and II, the two major types of camouflage were low visibility *blending* (which depended on extreme similarity) and *dazzle* (which depended on extreme difference). Blending is somewhat like silence, whereas dazzle is like confusing noise.

In blending camouflage, an object is concealed by making it highly similar to its background, so that two things appear to be one. In dazzle camouflage, contrasting erratic patterns are painted on the surface of the object, which make it appear to be a conglomeration of two or more distinctive shapes.

Blending camouflage is extreme unity without variety (all things seem like one thing). Dazzle camouflage is extreme variety without unity (one thing seems like many things). Astounding examples of these two types of camouflage are found in natural forms as well, in patterns on moth and butterfly wings, in the coloration of snakes, and so on. Many of the military camouflage schemes used in World Wars I and II were made by imitating camouflage patterns in nature.

Hodgepodge and Humdrum

Whether we know it or not, a major part of normal life consists of periodic struggles to avoid a kind of anesthetic existence. If you are at all like me, you have two major problems in life which constantly recur: First, there are certain days or weeks in which our life seems "all the same." Nothing is new and exciting. Time drags on. We say that life is *humdrum* (extreme similarity). We become bored or even depressed. We look around for new friends, escape to the movies, browse around in shopping malls, or look for stimulating books.

Second, there are other times when life seems overwhelming. Too many different things appear to be happening at the same time. People expect too much from us, and we "cannot get it together," we say. Time goes by too quickly, and life is like a *hodgepodge* (extreme difference). We become anxious. We run to friends for comfort. We dream about "the old days" and pick up former habits in hopes of making life more serene.

Humdrum forms of living are unity without variety. Hodgepodge forms are variety without unity. When we are "composed" in life, our pattern of experiences is a mixture of regularity and change, of harmony and discord. It is esthetic living. It is unity with variety.

CAMOUFLAGE Anesthetic patterns in nature, military constructions, secret codes, and elsewhere, which are designed in such a way that it is difficult to perceive the kind, location, and timing of an object or event.

DAZZLE CAMOUFLAGE Patterns of strongly contrasting shapes applied to the surface of an object in such a way that it is extremely difficult to see that object as one thing. It is variety without unity (extreme variation).

BLENDING CAMOUFLAGE Concealment patterns in which an object is made to appear so similar to its background or surroundings that it is no longer distinguishable as a separate thing. It is unity without variety (extreme repetition).

MIMICRY A special case of blending camouflage in which a thing is made to appear so similar to another *kind* of thing that it is likely to be mistaken for it (for example, certain butterflies have a remarkable resemblance to dead leaves).

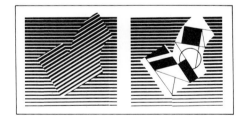

FIGURE 1-6 In blending camouflage (left diagram), the figure is concealed by making it highly similar to its background. In dazzle camouflage (right diagram), the figure tends to fall apart as contrasting erratic patterns cut across its surface, resulting in a "crazy quilt."

FIGURE 1-7 James Buckels. *House of Blue Leaves*. 1977. Gouache and ink, 10″ × 11½″. Private collection (originally published as theater poster illustration, University of Northern Iowa). The shocking presence of the boy is all the more disturbing in relation to the incessant repetition of the bird figures, especially the eyes and the beaks.

Or consider clothing styles. Well-dressed people tend to wear colors, styles, and textures of clothing that go together while also exhibiting contrasts. With the exception of uniforms and outlandish costumes, one would rarely ever see a person dressed completely in one color. Nor do well-dressed people wear an outrageous mixture of contrasting colors and textures. (There are, of course, exceptions, and fashion designers experiment with arrangements of extreme similarity and extreme difference whenever they want to be daring.)

Or think of ways that people move, their hand gestures and body postures, how they walk. When a person moves gracefully, each section of the body moves in such a manner that it is at the same time *similar to* and *different from* the movement of the total form. Arthur Koestler has called this phenomenon a *holon,* since it is an individual, a "whole" within itself, while at the very same time it is a "part" of a greater whole. Relationships of this sort have unity with variety. They are esthetic forms.

Some people have insisted that "healthy" states are characterized by unity with variety. For example, they point out that cancerous tissue is characterized by variety without unity, in that a cell begins to grow with seemingly no regard for the total body. People have also suggested that communities will decline when one of two conditions prevail: when individuals act only in their own interests, with little or no regard for the interests of the larger community (variety without unity), and when the larger community suppresses individuality, so that everyone conforms (unity without variety).

Similarity and Difference

Unity is the result of similarity, in that things which look alike appear to belong together. Variety is the result of difference, in that things which look unlike appear to belong apart. The recurring theme throughout this book, the thread of thought that runs throughout, is that our perception of *likeness* is the chief adhesive with which we put together life. Twenty-four hundred years ago, Aristotle talked about the importance of similarity in the logical classification of things. Twenty-three centuries later, the Gestalt psychologists tried to show that *similarity grouping* (the unit-forming factors, or principles of perceptual organization) is the fundamental glue in our comprehension of the kind, location, and timing of things.

As later chapters will explain, the essence of visual esthetic design is the precarious juggling of the similarities and differences among the visible features

. . . repetition is what holds life together. . . . A painting in which no line, no shape, no color, no size, no direction, no movement, was in any way ever repeated would be complete disorder.

Arthur B. Fallico, *Art and Existentialism* (Englewood Cliffs, N.J.: Prentice-Hall, 1962), p. 48.

Complexity without order produces confusion; order without complexity produces boredom.

Rudolf Arnheim, *Toward a Psychology of Art* (Berkeley: University of California Press, 1972), p. 124.

. . . we must ultimately be able to account for the most basic fact of aesthetic experience, the fact that delight lies somewhere between boredom and confusion.

Sir E. H. Gombrich, *The Sense of Order* (Ithaca, N.Y.: Cornell University Press, 1979), p. 9.

William James has defined genius as the capacity to see similarities in a background of differences, because under certain conditions it is extremely difficult for a person to perceive similarity in diversity. . . . Secret codes and camouflage take advantage of this fact.

H. G. Barnett, *Innovation: The Basis of Cultural Change* (New York: McGraw-Hill, 1953), p. 204.

of things—the lengths and thicknesses of lines; the value and brilliance of colors; the size and placement of shapes; the recurrence of rhythms, textures, proportions, orientations, and so on. Further, I will also show that what we call "creative acts" consist of new arrangements, a kind of perceptual reshuffling in which odd suits of cards are paired—a cognitive version of musical chairs.

As stated earlier, a work of art may be evaluated as "good" or "bad" on the basis of all sorts of criteria—technical, economic, narrative, innovative, and

FIGURE 1-8   David Bower. *Sheep Have No Fear Because of Their Whiteness.* 1980. Mixed media, 7″ × 10″ × 33″. Courtesy the artist and Roy Boyd Gallery, Los Angeles/ Chicago. There are deliberate applications of both low visibility (blending) and dazzle camouflage in this three-dimensional "shelf environment." Notice the repetition of stripes throughout the pattern on the wall and, in somewhat different form, on the various sticks and ropes.

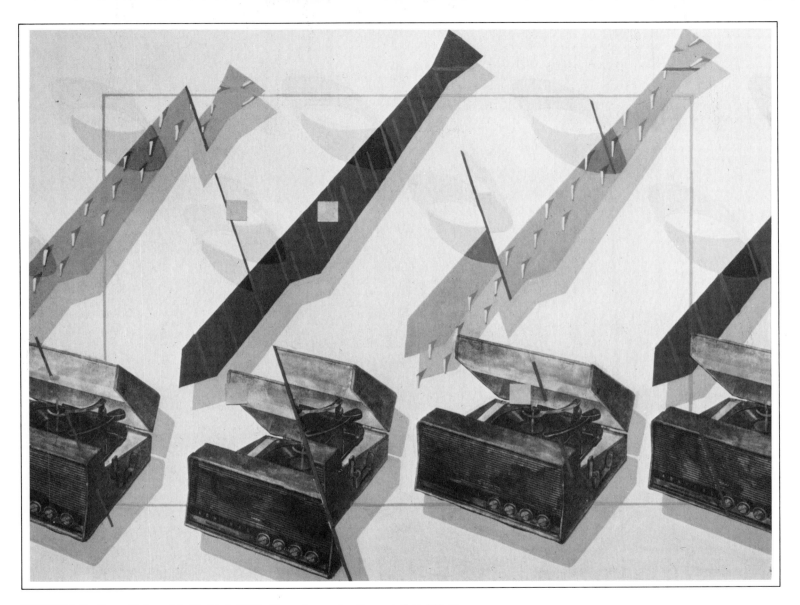

FIGURE 1-9 Scott Zukowski. *Untitled*. 1982. Gouache and collage, 14″ × 18″. Courtesy the artist (student, University of Wisconsin—Milwaukee). This is a witty solution to two-dimensional Problem Three, described in Chapter 6. As simple as its structure is, this is a marvelously complex arrangement which yields all sorts of surprises. Right of center, for example, a pattern of vertical strokes runs off the edge of the tie and flows into a shadow.

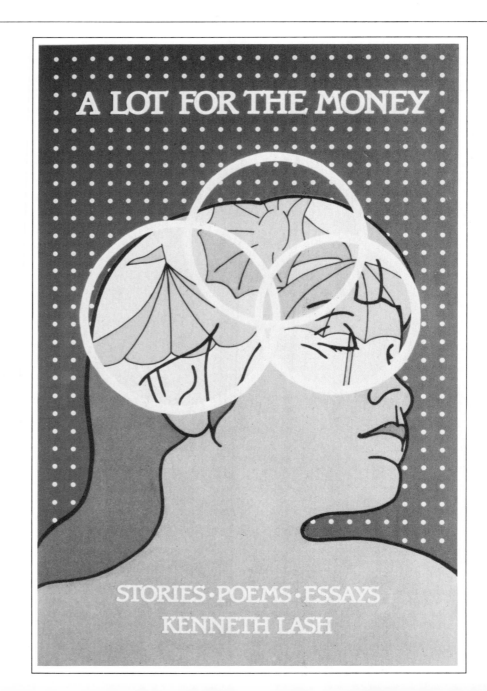

FIGURE 1-10 Jon Cisler. Book jacket proposal. 1982. Courtesy the artist (student, University of Wisconsin—Milwaukee). A woman's face, three rings, and various circus items are precariously overlapped in an illusion of transparency.

historical. However, when a work is a weak *esthetic* design, it fails for one of two reasons: Its features are characterized by too much similarity (unity with insufficient variety), or its features are characterized by too much difference (variety with insufficient unity).

One must always keep in mind that esthetic criteria (as are most that I know of) are only *approximate* yardsticks, since the ability of a viewer to perceive similarities and differences may vary with expectations, education, and experience. Further, the mind will naturally try to avoid anesthetic structures; it will try to see likeness in extremely dissimilar forms, and it will try to see differences in extremely monotonous forms.

Within works of visual art, the "proper" or optimum mixture of similarity and dissimilarity (of unity with variety) may vary somewhat in time by *taste*. But taste is not our chief concern, and art is not (as some would say) "all a matter of taste." There are dependable, albeit approximate, guidelines in terms of which designs are made.

Finally, we should realize that the most daring and inventive art of any time will probably tend to fall teasingly toward one extreme or the other. That is, it will attempt to be as unified as possible while still maintaining some surprising variety, or it will attempt to be as variegated as possible with the most daring and subtle unifying factors. Works which fall in the center are sometimes disdained by artists as being too safe or too easy.

One of the central pleasures of art is *making the hard look easy*. Artists for whom the criterion of unity with variety has become a too-rigid prescription are like tightrope walkers who lay their ropes across the floor. They do not take sufficient risks to make their works amazing. However, as a novice at visual esthetic design, you would be well-advised to practice on the floor at first.

Design is a means of ordering visual and emotional experience to give unity and consistency to a work of art. . . . Design is essentially visual control, and consciously or unconsciously the artist develops methods of ordering that are visually comprehensible.

R. L. Wickiser, "Design," in *Encyclopedia of World Art* (New York: McGraw-Hill, 1959), p. 356.

I do not take drugs. I am drugs.

Salvador Dali.

Chapter 2

Color and Context

Elements and Principles

Were this a conventional book on design, I would now present two lists. One would be a list of the so-called *elements of design,* which are usually said to be the structural features of works of art (psychologists would call them *grouping attributes*), such as line, texture, shape, color, and value. The second would be a list of certain *principles of design,* which are effects that can occur when those elements are combined—such as visual balance, economy of means, the illusion of movement, the dominance of focal points, proportional systems, and so on.

That is precisely how I was taught, but I don't think I learned that way. I learned visual esthetic design in much the same way that I learned how to ride a bicycle. True, I was told what wheels were for and where to grab the handle bars. But mostly I learned how to ride by watching others ride their bikes and (with a guiding push of course) jumping on and taking off.

While I was learning to ride, I fell down a lot at first, and several times I skinned my knees. But it was not long before I picked up the general idea—the

In painting, sculpture, and in fact in all the formative arts, in architecture and horticulture, so far as fine arts, the design *is what is essential. . . .*

Immanuel Kant.

ELEMENTS OF DESIGN Structural features of works of art (sometimes called *grouping attributes),* such as lines, textures, hues, values, intensities, shapes, and sizes. The similarity and dissimilarity among these traits determine the extent to which a work is called esthetic.

FIGURE 2-1   Steven Stocker. *Eclipse.* 1982. Collage, 14″ × 16″. Courtesy the artist (student, University of Wisconsin—Milwaukee). In this solution to two-dimensional Problem Two, the horizontal tubelike shape and the inverted repetitions of "eclipse" suggest a bilateral symmetry at the top, which is deftly offset by the diagonal band of pinstripes, one abandoned high-heeled shoe, and the surprising (but logical) juggling of squares. There is an asymmetry below because the figure is daringly shoved to the right.

total feeling—of what it meant to ride a bike. And it was only later, much later, that I had any interest in all the intricate parts of bikes, like pedals and spokes.

Despite the efforts of teachers to teach me the various "parts" of design (the elements and principles), I think I learned to "ride" design by looking at art that others had done and by simply "jumping on." I fell down a lot in art (I have a full spectrum of bruises), until I came to have a sense of what esthetic forms feel like. I still have a lot to learn, but there are days (and sometimes weeks) when I now ride without my hands or purposely ride over hurdles and ramps. In future years, I want to be even more daring.

PRINCIPLES OF DESIGN   Perceptual effects which can result (sometimes desired, sometimes not) from the combination of structural features, such as the illusion of movement, visual balance, the dominance of focal points, economy of means, and proportional systems.

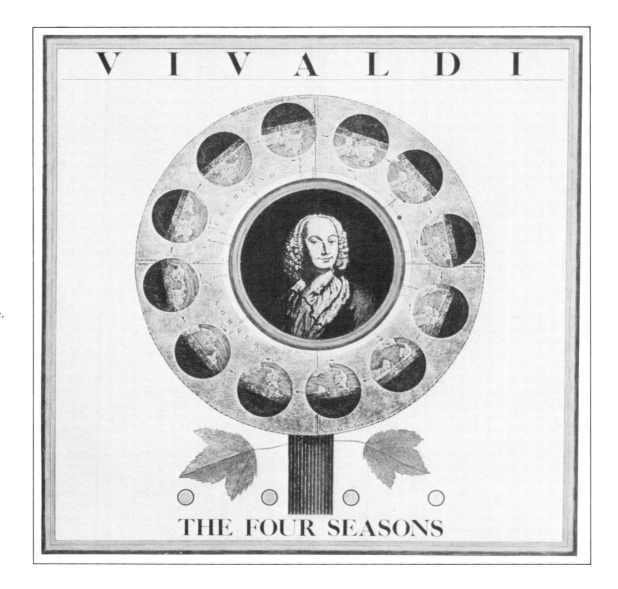

FIGURE 2-2 Brian Blanchette. Album cover design. 1981. Collage and mixed media, 12¼″ × 12¼″. Courtesy the artist (student, University of Wisconsin—Milwaukee). The central configuration has been shifted upward so that it does not coincide with the center of the square format. Within the larger circular form, there is a radial symmetry which helps the "picture" to convey the feeling of seasonal cycles. Circular forms are repeated throughout. Rich variety is ensured by the exaggerated extension of the letter spacing in "Vivaldi" and the delicate line below it.

In light of what I have just said, should this book be a "manual" of sorts, to tell you what wheels are the finest or how much air to fill them with or when and how to check your brakes? I hope not. I suspect you learn like me—by getting a general idea and by simply jumping on. I don't learn by listing parts. I learn by comprehending wholes.

In this chapter, I am asking that you mount a kind of bike called *color*. It isn't a terribly perilous feat, since I have added training wheels. However, you will also be riding on *context*, because (as it took me so long to find out) color is married to context; they are inseparable notions. I am choosing this approach because it seems to me that if you see how color works (as an element of design) in relation to context (as a principle of design), you will—with a smidgen of smartness—have some general feeling of how a work of art is made. Then, in subsequent chapters, I will try to fill the gaps. But be prepared to skin your knees.

I mix them with my brains, Sir.

John Opie (eighteenth-century British painter, when an amateur asked him how he mixed his colors).

The Key to Color

In terms of visual esthetic design, the key to using color is in the fact that it can be *changed* or modified.

By understanding this, it is entirely possible to make intelligent and inventive uses of color within works of visual art, with little or no understanding of "color notation systems," such as those of Wilhelm Ostwald and Alfred H. Munsell, although systems of this sort can be immensely helpful.

To put it simply, the modification of colors enables visual artists to accomplish two things: to make *different* colors appear to be similar, and to make *similar* colors appear to be different. Color, like everything else in life, depends on the process of *sorting*.

When different colors are made to look similar, the *unity* of a work of art is increased because of the increase in similarity. When similar colors are made to look different, *variety* is increased because of the increase in difference.

Accordingly, the modification of colors is a major means by which artists can avoid the anesthetic conditions of monotony (extreme similarity) and chaos (extreme difference) and thus be able to achieve the esthetic requirement of unity with variety within a work of visual art.

Colors can be modified in two major ways: by the mixture of pigments and by simultaneous contrast. There are other ways as well—for example, we can

COLOR MODIFICATIONS Alterations in the appearance of a color, usually brought about in art by mixing two colors together or by simultaneous contrast. These changes are important because they determine the extent to which colors are perceived as similar or different, which may in turn determine whether a work is characterized by unity with variety.

SORTING Processes in thinking and perceiving by which we determine the kind, location, and timing of things. In general, those things which are perceived as (or thought to be) similar are seen as belonging together, whereas those which are dissimilar are seen as belonging apart. Sometimes this process is also called *categorization* or *grouping*. All human activity depends on a process of sorting.

FIGURE 2-3 Christine Mercado. *Untitled.* 1980. Collage and gouache, 10″ × 14″. Courtesy the artist (student, University of Wisconsin—Milwaukee). Surprising inconsistencies make this work intriguing. The stripes on the right side are slightly diagonal. The negative space between two stripes (directly right of the bottom center) has become a positive shape. The line which crosses the circular form works both as an accent to shape and as a teasing pictorial clue, since it may remind us of surface eruptions on the sun, a cracked egg, or the oscilloscopic record of a birdsong.

apply paint to surfaces of varying smoothness, or we can dim or change the light under which the paint is viewed.

The Mixing of Pigments

There are four common ways by which colors can be modified by the mixture of pigments:

1. We can add one hue to another hue. *Hue* is the common technical name for the chroma or color itself. The *primary* hues are usually (not always) said to be yellow, blue, and red, in accordance with a system for grouping pigment hues, invented in 1730, called the *color wheel*. It is an arbitrary system (as is any grouping scheme), which has advantages and flaws. For various technical reasons, other color grouping schemes have used other basic hues. The Munsell system, for example, considers five hues as basic (green and purple are listed as primaries), whereas Ostwald's scheme is based on four.

Within the traditional color wheel (which is adequate for the purposes of most artists), yellow, blue, and red are said to be primary hues because they cannot be produced by mixing other pigments. That is, we have to start with them. They are also primary because it is commonly thought that by mixing these three hues, we can produce all other hues. In fact, this is not strictly true (some exceptions have been found), but that need not concern us.

When two primary hues are mixed in approximately equal proportions, blue and red will produce violet, red and yellow will produce orange, and blue and yellow will produce green. The three hues which result are commonly referred to as *secondary hues*.

We need not stop there, of course. Any primary hue can also be mixed with a secondary hue on either side of it, in which case we would produce an array of six tertiary or *intermediate hues*, such as yellow orange, blue green, red violet, and so on.

It should also be obvious that we need not be restricted to mixing only hues which are next to each other on the color wheel. Indeed, we could mix two (or three or more) hues which are widely separated.

Hues which are most widely separated (directly opposite from one another) on the color wheel are referred to as *complementary hues*. They are generally thought to be most different from one another, so that when juxtaposed they can be made to engage in a high-pitched optical quarreling bout.

HUE   The chromatic attribute of color. The hues within a spectrum are traditionally listed as red, orange, yellow, green, blue, indigo, and violet. Black and white (and grays produced by mixing the two) are not commonly labeled hues.

PRIMARY HUES   Red, yellow, and blue. They are called primary because (it is usually said) they cannot be produced by mixing other hues and because all other hues can be made by mixing these three hues.

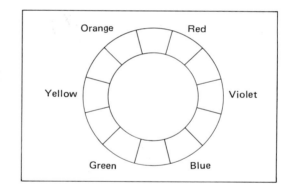

FIGURE 2-4   The traditional color wheel (see Color Plate 1).

SECONDARY HUES   Orange, green, and violet. These are produced by mixing approximately equal amounts of two primary hues. Red plus yellow equals orange. Yellow plus blue equals green. Blue plus red equals violet.

INTERMEDIATE HUES Red orange, red violet, blue violet, blue green, yellow green, and yellow orange. Sometimes called *tertiary hues,* they are produced by mixing a primary hue with an adjacent secondary hue.

COMPLEMENTARY HUES Any two hues which are most widely separated on the color wheel. Red is the complement of green. Blue is the complement of orange.

NEUTRAL HUES Hues which have been "toned down" (lessened in vividness or purity) by being mixed with nonhue gray or by being mixed with complementary hues.

TINT Any hue to which any amount of white has been added.

SHADE Any hue to which any amount of black has been added.

TONE Any hue to which any amount of nonhue gray has been added or any amount of its complement.

VALUE The "lightness" of a color. Changes in value are produced by adding white or black to any hue. Value is increased by the addition of white. Value is decreased by the addition of black.

INTENSITY The "brightness" (purity or vividness) of a hue. Changes in intensity are produced by adding nonhue gray of the same value to any hue or by mixing the hue with its complementary hue.

As will be discussed in a moment, hues are often made "low key" (reduced in vividness or pitch) by the artist mixing two complementaries, rather than placing them side by side. The mixtures which result are commonly labeled *neutral hues.* Most hues that are normally classed as brown or gray (as distinct from nonhue gray) are produced by mixing varying amounts of complementary hues or by mixing other hues which are widely separated on the color wheel.

2. We can add white to any hue, the result of which is called a *tint.* White and black are "colors," but they are not considered hues because they have no chroma.

Two different hues can be made to appear similar by adding white to both (these are sometimes called *pastels*). Two samples of the same hue can be made to appear different by adding white to only one or by adding different amounts.

3. We can add black to any hue, the result of which is called a *shade.* Two different hues can be made to appear similar by adding black to both. Two samples of the same hue can be made to appear different by adding black to only one or by adding different amounts.

4. We can add gray (a mixture of black and white) to any hue, the result of which is called a *tone.* Two different hues can be made to appear similar by adding nonhue gray to both. Two samples of the same hue can be made to appear different by adding gray to only one or by adding different amounts.

Value and Intensity

Modifications in the "quantity of lightness" of a color are commonly referred to as changes in its *value.* When white or black (and sometimes gray) are added to hues, changes in value are produced. When white is added to a hue, we say that its value is "higher." When black is added, we say that its value is "lower."

Modifications in the "quality" (or purity) of a hue are usually referred to as changes in *intensity.* These are also often called changes in saturation, chroma, or tone, depending on the book we read. The terms may seem confusing, but similar variances in terminology occur in virtually any activity that we may elect to pursue, so this should not surprise us. The important point to know is that modifications in intensity result in a kind of "dulling" of hues. Hues are usually "toned down" by mixing a hue with a nonhue gray of *the same value as the hue* (so that the value remains the same) or by mixing the hue with small amounts of its complement (for example, adding red to green). Thus, two different hues can be

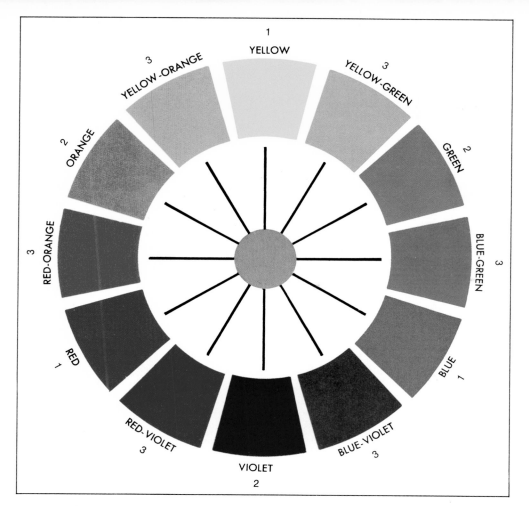

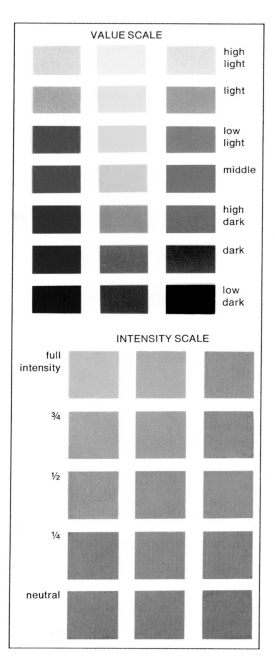

COLORPLATE 1 Traditional color wheel. The common assumption that there are three primary hues (red, yellow, and blue), which in the mixture of pigments produce all other colors, appears to have been first proposed in 1730 by J. C. Le Blon, a German engraver. Secondary hues (orange, green, and violet) are made by mixing two primaries. Intermediate or tertiary hues (yellow orange, yellow green, blue green, blue violet, red violet, and red orange) result from mixtures of adjacent primaries and secondaries. The gray or brown at the hub of the wheel is the neutralized mixture of all three primaries.

COLORPLATE 2 Value and intensity scales. Changes in value result when either white or black are added to a hue. Intensity changes occur by adding nonhue middle gray or adding the complement of the hue.

COLORPLATE 3 Design and color in various butterfly forms. Collection of the author.

COLORPLATE 4 Susan Miles. *New Vistas.* 1980. Watercolor, 25″ X 40″. Collection of Pillsbury Company, Minneapolis. Courtesy the artist. The predominant colors in this work are either cool (blue and green) or neutral (black, white, and gray), with modified red as an accent. The symmetry is broken when the foreground structure is shifted toward the right and by irregular details, especially diagonal shadows and changes in the background trees.

COLORPLATE 5 Leslie Loomis Vansen. *Monkey Puzzle.* 1976. Acrylic, 61″ X 70″. Private collection. This is a remarkably venturesome work since rarely would an artist dare to use such widely differing hues. Yet because of reverberating shapes, delicate placements of tones and tints, and an intricate background space, the work remains a complex whole.

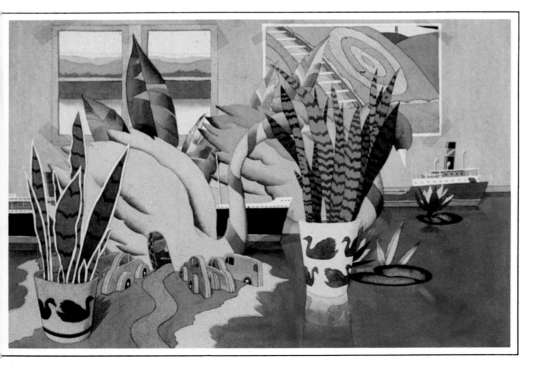

COLORPLATE 6 Brian Paulson. *The Queen Was Here.* 1980. Watercolor, 9¼″ X 13⅝″. Collection of Ozark Paper Company. Courtesy the artist. The predominant hues are blue and green, with small amounts of modified orange and intense red as accents. The stripes which climb the swan's neck are an apt allusion to horizontal background stripes as well as the stripes on the plants.

COLORPLATE 7 Stephen Samerjan. *Dogon Garden #9*. 1980–1981. Oil, 72″ X 105″. Courtesy the artist. This is an elaborate diptych, two canvases joined together as one. It is a virtue of the work that the two adjoining halves are disturbingly unequal (the right side is slightly wider than the left), which complicates the symmetry. This is a clear example of an analogous color scheme (yellow, orange, and red) with shocking intrusions of green.

COLORPLATE 8 Alicia Czechowski. *Furious Slaughter III*. 1981. Pastel, 30″ X 40″. Courtesy the artist. If this work is disturbing, it is in part the consequence of the rawness of the pastel strokes, the predominance of red, and the oblique angle from which the symmetrical figures are viewed. A metaphor may be implied in which there is a link between intimacy and violence, between tranquility and death.

COLORPLATE 9 Amy Marein. *Elbereth.* 1981. Mixed media, 20″ X 27″. Private collection. There is a complex tension here between the highly formal geometric squares and grids and the gauzy, ephemeral faces.

COLORPLATE 10 John Colt. *Journey to the East.* 1972. Acrylic, 64½″ X 72″. Private collection. This artist is intrigued by Haitian and other "primitive" art, in which frequent use is made of bilateral symmetry, broken by maverick details. The hue scheme is analogous (orange and yellow), accented by blue in the center and by green around the edge.

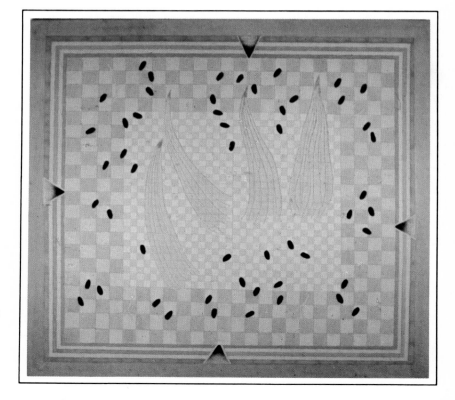

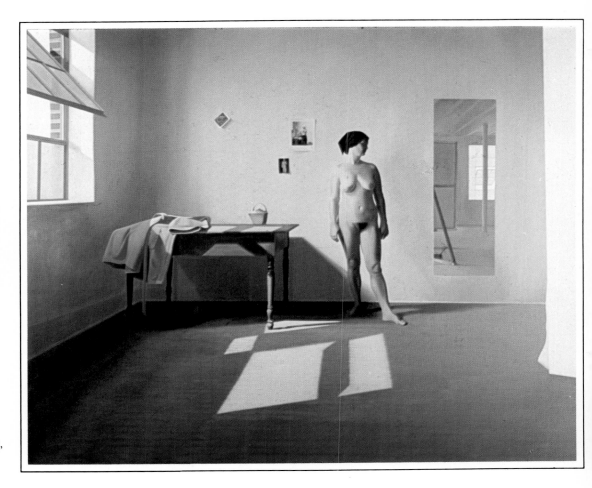

COLORPLATE 11 John Lofton. *Bird-Cage*. 1976. Mixed media construction, interior 8½″ X 20¼″ X 30″, exterior height with base 7′7″. Courtesy the artist. The red bill on the figure's cap accents the predominant green of the room. By the placement of the light, lost-and-found contours occur. The pictorial meaning of the work is clouded and perplexing. Why is the bird perched on a stick? Why is the boy on the stairs? Where does the ceiling trapdoor lead?

COLORPLATE 12 Steven E. Bigler. *Studio*. 1978–1980. Oil, 66″ X 82½″. Courtesy the artist. This is a highly structured work in which every detail seems to be perfectly placed. Compare the angle of the model's diagonal leg with that of the leg of the easel reflected in the mirror. Note the correspondence between the window's bottom edge and that of the window in the mirror, the correlation of the shadows on the floor with the upright leg of the figure, the gestural resemblance between the lighted table leg and the model's upright leg, and so on.

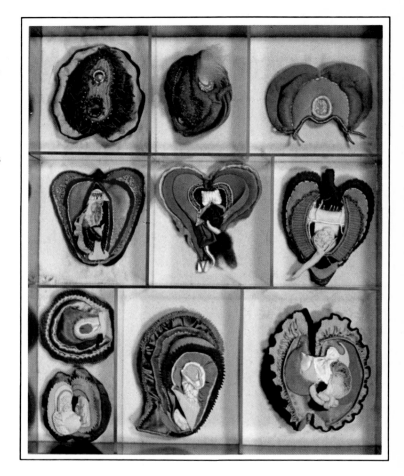

COLORPLATE 13 Ruth Kao. *Forbidden Miniatures.* 1977. Stuffed fabric with stitchery, encased in plexiglas with sand, 3″ X 16″ X 13″. Courtesy the artist. This shellfish menagerie, by a Chinese-born American fiber artist, was inspired by a nineteenth-century German zoological print of the interior parts of ocean forms. There is an allusion to sexual taboo and to the "forbidden stitch," a Chinese sewing knot which was reputedly so small that upper-class unmarried women were forbidden to use it, for fear that it would harm their sight and spoil their chances to marry.

COLORPLATE 14 Robert L. Grilley. *Eli and Juneko Sleeping.* 1978. Oil, 40″ X 50″. Courtesy the artist. This is an approximate use of a direct complementary color scheme, in that the foreground orange is poised against the background blue. The small amounts of violet (in the upper right corner and in the foreground hat) serve as vibrant accents, as does the singular green at left. The breathtaking richness of the work is in large part due to the intricate patches of patterns.

COLORPLATE 15 John Balsley. *Er . . . Um, He Recollected That Kinetic Memory Was Just . . . Um.* 1981–1982. Mixed media, 18½″ X 19″ X 33½″. Courtesy the artist and Frumkin-Struve Gallery, Chicago. The title is marvelously fitting for this bizarre, perturbing work. The spherical and linear repetitions are clearly evident, but the mind is poked and probed (the tossing and turning of closure) to interpret what it means.

COLORPLATE 16 David Bower. *There and Elsewhere.* 1979. Mixed media construction, 7″ X 10″ X 24″. Collection of Robert Fields, Chicago. Courtesy the artist and Roy Boyd Gallery, Los Angeles/Chicago. The artist has ingeniously combined perplexing surreal miniature walls with patterns from military camouflage schemes. Notice the red accent above the central table shape and the intricate fragmentation of the window, sticks, and table as the two large patterns merge.

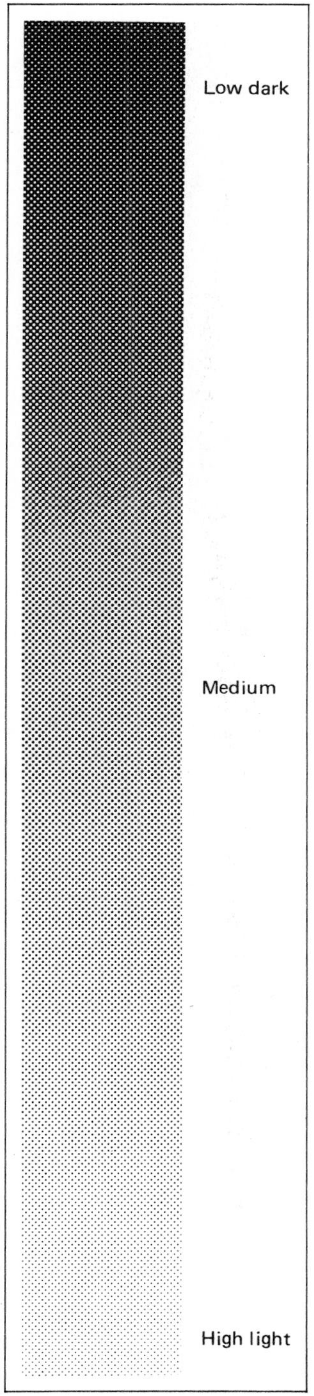

Low dark

Medium

High light

FIGURE 2-5 The gradation of value, achieved by mixing black with white (see Color Plate 2).

FIGURE 2-6 Jon Cisler. *Edith's Dead.* 1982. Collage and mixed media, 11″ × 15″. Courtesy the artist (student, University of Wisconsin—Milwaukee). This is a solution to two-dimensional Problem Two, described in Chapter 6. The owllike appearance of the human figure is amusingly reflected by the gogglelike eyes of the owls. Notice the playful handling of the horizontal pinstripes, which lie in front at certain times and yet fall back at other times.

made to appear similar by giving them the same intensity. Or two samples of the same hue can be made to appear different by giving them different intensities.

Color Notation Systems

COLOR NOTATION SYSTEMS Schematic systems for displaying, arranging, and labeling a large number of hues, tints, shades, and tones, obtained through the mixture of pigments. They are of use to artists because they allow access to an unimaginable range of color modifications.

Artists can color the sky red because they know it's blue. Those of us who aren't artists must color things the way they really are or people might think we're stupid.
Jules Feiffer, *Crawling Arnold.*

Anyone who sees and paints a sky green and pastures blue ought to be sterilized.
Adolf Hitler.

There are certain times in life when colors are purposely made to clash; that is, they are designed to be as different from each other as possible. We can predictably make them clash by juxtaposing colors which are not only widely disparate in hues but also in values and intensities.

There are other times in life when colors are selected to be confusingly alike. We can predictably make them blend by juxtaposing colors which are the same or very alike in terms of all three attributes—hue, value, and intensity.

Visual esthetic design, as we said, prospers on a balanced meal of similarity and difference, of unity *with* variety. It would seem to follow then that esthetic arrangements would probably use combinations of colors which are alike in certain ways (unity) but markedly different in other respects (variety). For example, we might use vastly different hues with similar values and intensities. Or we may use colors of similar values and hues with distinctly different intensities. At the risk of making rules, some people have even suggested that "harmonious" colors are probably best if they are highly similar in terms of *two* of the attributes (hue, value, or intensity) but remarkably different in *one*.

Whatever the colors we choose, it is impossible for anyone to imagine the enormous range of color variations that can readily be produced by modifications of hue, value, and intensity. The importance of color notation systems (with hundreds of samples of modified hues), like those of Ostwald and Munsell, is that they allow us to see, locate, name, and determine the ingredients of a large selection of modified hues within a consistent grouping scheme. These systems catalog and show a far greater number of possible hues than we can name or even think. The Munsell system alone contains 1,200 modifications, whereas it is sometimes said that the average person is readily familiar with and can readily name only about eighteen or twenty colors.

Simultaneous Contrast

There is a second major way by which colors can be modified which does not depend on the mixing of pigments. Colors can be modified in appearance simply by changing their backgrounds. This is called *simultaneous contrast.*

The term was coined in 1839 by Michel Eugène Chevreul, a French chemist who had been appointed the director of the dyeing department of the Royal Gobelin Manufacturers in Paris. The concept had been recognized and used for centuries by artists, but Chevreul was the first to analyze and describe it thoroughly.

Chevreul's discovery came about because he received complaints about the inconsistency of colors in the fibers of certain tapestries. To his surprise, he found that these color differences were not attributable to defects in the dyes. Rather, two samples of the same fibers appeared to be two different colors when placed on different backgrounds.

More specifically, Chevreul discovered that a patch of nonhue gray appeared to be lighter when placed on a black background and darker when placed on a white background. This is now referred to as the *simultaneous contrast of value*.

He also discovered (and this is especially amazing) that a patch of nonhue gray appeared to be slightly red if placed on a green background (the complement of red), whereas it appeared to be slightly green if placed on a red background.

Further, he discovered that a patch of red will appear to be more intensely red when placed on a green background, whereas it will appear to be less intense when placed on background colors which are next to it on the color wheel. These are examples of the *simultaneous contrast of hues*.

In these and other examples, the changes which result from simultaneous contrast can be much more startling than we might first imagine; they can in fact be so pronounced that they seem to be magical changes.

Chevreul published a long list of the specific effects of simultaneous contrast. However, if we carefully think about the examples previously mentioned, it should be evident that there is one general principle which all these modifications share: Whenever two colors are placed directly next to each other, their differences will be heightened or (to use a loaded word) *accentuated*.

The precise reason for simultaneous contrast remains somewhat of a mystery still, but surely it must derive in part from the fact that things are known and judged by being *compared* with other things; that is, we know things by their contexts. For that reason, artists sometimes photograph works with a familiar object (an egg or maybe a ruler) beside them, so that the scale of the work can be seen in relation to the size of a thing that everyone knows.

In the same way that works of art can only be judged "good" or "bad" in relation to certain intentions, a color can only be judged as "more red" or "less red" in relation to its background or surroundings.

SIMULTANEOUS CONTRAST Alterations in the appearance of a color caused by changing its background or surroundings. The resulting modifications are somewhat predictable, in that when things are juxtaposed their differences will be heightened.

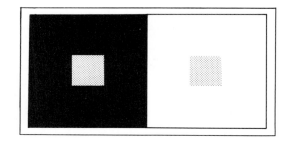

FIGURE 2-7 In the simultaneous contrast of value, two samples of the same gray appear to be lighter when placed on a black background and darker when placed on a white background.

A sallow color makes another which is placed next to it appear to be more lively, and melancholy and pallid colors enable those beside them to seem very cheerful and of a flaming brilliance.
Giorgio Vasari.

When red is next to green or blue, they render each other more handsome and vivid.
Leon Battista Alberti.

FIGURE 2-8   Frank Sikora. *Come Home, Natassia*. 1982. Collage and mixed media, 8½″ × 14″. Courtesy the artist (student, University of Wisconsin—Milwaukee). In this response to two-dimensional Problem Two, there is a repetition of threes, sometimes occurring in groups of three. The relatively simple structure is sufficiently enriched by the careful shifting of the rocks, easels, portraits, and so on, away from the central axis.

Observations of this sort have led some people to conclude that everything is relative. This statement seems true to a great extent, since everything is relative to a context; but once the context has been fixed, further judgements need not be relative. For example, if we decide that a certain red will always be placed on the same background, it will (everything else being equal) always appear to be the same red.

Successive Contrast

Chevreul distinguished simultaneous contrast from successive contrast, or what is more commonly called the phenomenon of *afterimages*.

An afterimage can be seen very simply by staring at any color (or any assembly of colors) for about a minute, then quickly shifting our gaze to a blank white background. A ghostlike image of the original shape will appear on the white surface, but in a hue or value which is the approximate complement of the original color.

Successive contrast is of considerable interest to physiologists. In terms of visual esthetic design, however, it is of little importance in art.

SUCCESSIVE CONTRAST An optical phenomenon which can be produced by staring at a patch of color for about a minute, then switching our gaze to a white background. A ghostlike image of the original patch—but in its complementary color—will appear briefly on the white background. This is commonly referred to as an *afterimage.*

Color Interaction

The phenomenon of simultaneous contrast is not limited to color. As demonstrated by various optical illusions, there can be simultaneous contrast of size and shape. It is conceivable that some kind of simultaneous contrast can be perceived between any two things that are juxtaposed.

That the simultaneous contrast of color is usually stressed is probably due to the writings of two teachers, Johannes Itten and Josef Albers. At different times, each was in charge of the beginning design courses at the most influential art school of this century, the German *Bauhaus*. Opened in 1919, the school was closed in 1933, when police and storm troopers arrested the few remaining students under the pretext that the Bauhaus had printed and distributed Communist literature and that, by its teaching, it was a "breeding ground of Bolshevism."

The Bauhaus was a breeding ground, but not of Bolshevist art. Rather, as its founder Walter Gropius (the prominent architect) declared in the school's

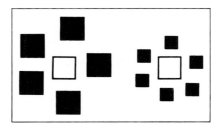

FIGURE 2-9 In this example of the simultaneous contrast of size, the central shapes in the two diagrams appear to be different sizes, even though, by measurement, they are precisely the same size.

BAUHAUS The most influential art school of the twentieth century, established with government funding by the architect Walter Gropius in Weimar, Germany, in 1919. In general, the school stressed the value of visual esthetic design in the making of functional objects.

We have no Art—we do everything well.
Statement attributed to the Balinese.

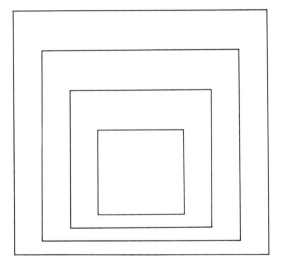

FIGURE 2-10 In Josef Albers' *Homage to the Square* paintings, on which this diagram is based, the strength of the shapes is weakened because of the repetition of squares, while the interaction of color is maximized.

I like painting on a square because you don't have to decide whether it should be longer-longer or shorter-shorter or longer-shorter; it's just a square.
Andy Warhol.

first proclamation, it called for the unification of the visual arts under the primacy of architecture. More important, it tried to stress the value of visual esthetic design in the construction of functional objects. Its impact was primarily caused by the uncommon strength of its teachers, including such well-known artists as Paul Klee, Wassily Kandinsky, Gerhard Marcks, Marcel Breuer, and Laszlo Moholy-Nagy.

Johannes Itten, who was dismissed from the Bauhaus in part because of his mystical beliefs (including, among other things, a diet which emphasized garlic) and unconventional teaching methods, was the author of *Design and Form* and *The Art of Color*. Albers (Itten's successor), who left Germany in the 1920s to teach at Black Mountain College and Yale, was the author of *The Interaction of Color*. These three books, the clarity and usefulness of which are somewhat controversial, have been enormously influential.

Albers is of interest here because the paintings which established his reputation as a major artist are primarily experiments with simultaneous contrast and related color phenomena. These paintings, entitled *Homage to the Square*, depict colored squares placed on increasingly larger squares but shifted toward the bottom of the painting.

Despite their title, Albers' paintings do not pay homage to squares because (through simultaneous contrast of shape) their almost unvaried repetition weakens the vividness of that shape. His paintings pay homage to color. Attention is shifted away from the redundant squares and toward the changes in color (which is where the changes in information are), in which modifications occur through simultaneous contrast as the widths of the borders are varied.

As a teacher and author, Albers developed a series of exercises using colored papers in which he demonstrated (among other things), as Chevreul predicted, that (1) two samples of the same hue can be made to appear to be two different hues, and (2) two different hues can be made to appear to be the same hue. Some of his examples exhibit remarkable changes.

Color Depth and Temperature

Through both simultaneous contrast and the mixing of pigments, Albers' *Homage* paintings often show surprising illusions of depth, in which colors appear to be located at different distances from the eye (even though, in fact, they have been applied to the same surface).

FIGURE 2-11 Amy Marein. *Valentine for Rebecca.* 1981. Mixed media, 14½″ × 17½″. Private collection. Squares recur throughout this work, but they are sufficiently cloaked that the underlying grid is neither obvious nor obtrusive. The implied formal divisions contrast with and accent the more spontaneous lines and shapes.

COLOR DEPTH   The common visual illusion that different hues and values appear to lie at different distances from the eye, even though they are applied to the same surface. When a color "advances," it appears to lie in front of the surface. When a color "recedes," it appears to lie in back of the surface.

COLOR TEMPERATURE   The somewhat vague sensation that different hues convey different qualities of emotional intensity or temperature. Red, orange, and yellow are generally said to be "warm," and green, blue, and violet are generally said to be "cool."

When in doubt, wear red.
Bill Blass.

When in doubt, sing loud.
Robert Merrill.

ACCENT   An element of difference which through simultaneous contrast heightens or "accentuates" the distinctive characteristics of the predominant features of any structure. Accents are usually of small amount and, at least in terms of some attributes, remarkably different from the features which they heighten. In the same sense, a pinch of salt is added to steak to accent (to make more vivid) its distinctive taste.

Depth is yet another way by which similar colors can be made dissimilar and vice versa. The terms used for this phenomenon are *advancement* and *recession*. When a color advances, it appears to float in front of the surface on which it is painted. When a color recedes, it appears to lie beyond that surface. Advancement can be caused by the addition of white to any hue, and recession can be caused by the addition of black.

Artists also commonly say that hues themselves (without the addition of black and white) appear to be located at different distances from the eye. Those hues which are "warm" (yellow, orange, red) are generally seen as advancing, whereas those which are "cool" (violet, blue, green) are generally seen as receding.

When artists speak of hues as being "warm" or "cool," they are alluding to a vague sensation of emotional temperature or intensity. The validity of that sensation would be difficult to verify, but whatever its basis, it is frequently and successfully used in clothing design, packaging, and all sorts of advertising. A glance at a shelf of cigarette cartons will confirm, with some exceptions, that "tough-guy" brands of cigarettes are usually packaged in warm hues (red) and menthol brands in cool hues (green), whereas the cigarettes of those who think of themselves as "sophisticated" are packaged in neutral or nonhue colors (brown, gray, silver) with more complex, polysyllabic brand names. Some people have contended that there is a similar correlation between personality and the styles and colors of clothing.

How Accents Work

It was earlier stated that the primary effect of simultaneous contrast is the "accentuation" of differences. That word was purposely chosen because it is related to the common idea of *accent*.

People are implying the concept of accent when they say that variety is the spice of life. In cooking, spices are used as accents. By adding slight amounts of salt, we can accentuate or heighten the distinctive flavor, or "steakness," of a piece of steak.

There are at least two conditions which characterize an accent: It is usually greatly *different* from the thing with which it is combined (the taste of salt is radically different from that of steak), and it is used in amounts considerably *smaller* than the amount of the thing with which it is combined (we do not add a pound of salt to a pound of steak).

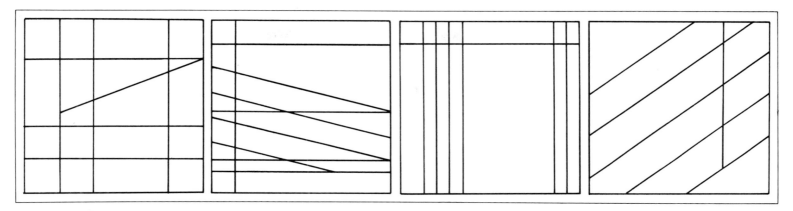

FIGURE 2-12 Accents can occur without the use of color. In these diagrams, a diagonal axis accents a system of horizontals and verticals, a vertical axis accents a system of horizontals and diagonals, and so on.

The use of an accent in cooking is precisely analogical to its use in visual esthetic design. Just as a pinch of salt will enliven the flavor of steak, so a fleck of green will enhance the "redness" of a work which consists primarily of warm hues.

It was probably this understanding which led to certain kinds of "underpainting," in which shapes which are intended to be colored might first be painted in a hue radically different from the intended final hue (for example, shapes intended to be red are first painted in green). The shapes can then be "overpainted" with the final hue, but with sufficient casualness that tittles of the first remain. It is believed that this practice (through simultaneous contrast) will accentuate the predominant hue.

If simultaneous contrast can be observed between any two things that are juxtaposed, it is logical to assume that accents can be made without the use of color. Thus, a horizontal line can accent a system of vertical lines. A diagonal line can accent a grid of horizontal and vertical lines. A circle can accent a pattern of squares. Tall can accent short. Large can accent small. Slow can accent fast. Soft can accent hard. Deliberate forms can accent more expressive forms. Loud can accent quiet. And so on.

In the coloration of Western art and clothing, it *may* be (and this is controversial) most common to find a group of cool or neutral hues being employed as

A kiss without a moustache is like an egg without salt.
M. J. Cawein.

Wit is the salt of conversation, not the food.
William Hazlitt.

predominant hues, with accents of red or orange. But there are major styles of art which have purposely violated this scheme, such as the widespread use of intense red in certain paintings of fauvists and expressionists, in pop art, or again, in optical art, where equal amounts of intense complementaries are frequently juxtaposed.

However, should this generalization be true, there are people who would say that cool hues are predominant in Western art because we live in surroundings which are themselves predominantly blue (sky) and green (trees and grass). But cultures which live in similar surroundings seem to have vastly different traditions. For example, one finds a common predominance of red in Chinese and Balinese color schemes (look at the color in the interiors of Chinese restaurants).

Color Schemes

COLOR SCHEMES General systematic plans for the selection and distribution of color (hues, values, and intensities) within any structure. An infinite number could be proposed. No color scheme is inherently more esthetic than any other.

LOCAL COLOR In picture-making, the selection and placement of colors so that the objects depicted are shown in the colors (hues, values, and intensities) they are commonly thought to have.

ARBITRARY COLOR In picture-making, the selection and placement of colors so that the objects depicted are shown in colors which have little or nothing to do with their conventional appearance (for example, a red hat colored as if it were green). Arbitrary color is often referred to as *subjective color,* although such uses of color need not necessarily be either subjective or arbitrary.

There are countless reasons for selecting a particular combination of colors (hues, values, and intensities) rather than choosing another. There are emotional reasons. There are goals and choices which have historical meaning. There are reasons which are scientific, psychological, nostalgic, narrative, religious, inventive, and so on. Color combinations can be sensibly chosen for all sorts of values and goals other than visual esthetic design.

We might favor certain hues because of their connections with certain objects or events (for example, the red, white, and blue of the American flag), or they might remind us of certain childhood events (the orange and black of Halloween). They may be chosen on the basis of their symbolic significance (white is the color of weddings, black the ancient sign for death). They could be selected on the basis of emotive tone or temperament (we "see red" when angry, "turn green" with envy, or "feel blue" when sad). They could be carefully chosen on the basis of optical visibility (yellow on black is a highly visible combination). But once again, these reasons may have little or nothing to do with visual esthetic design.

There are artists who select certain combinations of colors to comply with a highly deliberate plan or what is called a *color scheme.* There are other artists who work in a much more intuitive way, although when they have finished, their works may show a plan or scheme. It would be absurd to insist that one approach is always better than the other, and most of us probably employ both.

Color schemes, whether preconceived or not, are general plans or systems for categorizing the kinds and proportions of color in any particular work. There are, as we have mentioned, certain purposes for which one kind of color scheme is preferable to another (high visibility, for example, or maximum color vibration). In terms of visual esthetic design, it may be safe to say that no particular system or scheme is necessarily better than any other. Whatever scheme we choose, the colors (hues, values, and intensities) are changed and juxtaposed so that they are alike in some ways (unity) and markedly different in other respects (variety). We could succeed or fail in this requirement, whatever scheme is preconceived. Any scheme could be employed, since colors can be made to be similar or dissimilar by modification. Any two hues can be made to go together. Any two samples of one hue can be made to fall apart.

It is convenient, whether or not it is useful, to think of various schemes for hues as existing on a scale which extends from high difference (or low similarity) at one extreme to low difference (or high similarity) at the other.

In a *monochromatic* scheme, only a single hue is used, with modifications of value and intensity. In a strict *analogous* scheme, there are a limited number of hues (most often said to be three) which are next to one another on the color

I put down my colors without a preconceived plan. If at the first step and perhaps without my being conscious of it one tone has particularly pleased me, more often than not when the picture is finished I will notice that I have respected this tone while I have progressively altered and transformed the others. I discover the quality of colors in a purely instinctive way.

Henri Matisse, "Notes of a Painter" in *Henri-Matisse* (New York: Museum of Modern Art and W. W. Norton, 1931).

FIGURE 2-13 In a monochromatic color scheme, (a), only a single hue is employed. In an analogous scheme, (b), three adjacent hues are used. In a triadic scheme, (c), three equally distant hues are used. In split complementary systems, (d), a hue is juxtaposed with the hues which are on each side of its direct complement. In a direct complementary scheme, (e), two complementary hues are employed.

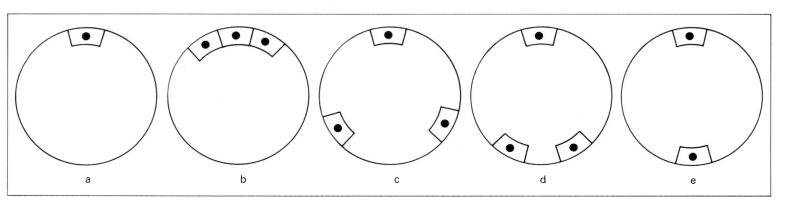

FIGURE 2-14 John Lofton. *Abandoned Nest in an Empty Room.* 1976. Wood and other media, interior 16″ × 28″ × 22″, exterior height with base 90″. Private collection. This is an exquisitely detailed miniature room. Simulated outdoor light shines behind the window shade. The desolate space in the foreground heightens the conspicuousness of the "nest" of background features. Perhaps the diagonal telephone cord is a taut reminder of affective tension or of desperate attempts to contact things beyond oneself.

FIGURE 2-15   Joe Sutter. Album cover design. 1981. Photograph and mixed media, 12¼″ × 12¼″. Courtesy the artist (student, University of Wisconsin—Milwaukee). This is a precarious balancing act, based on the juxtaposition of pairs. When the horizon is tilted to the left (as if the trees were pulling it down), it is counteracted when "Bad Boy" and "Youthful Adventures" are shifted toward the right.

wheel (yellow, green, and blue, for example). At least in terms of hue, these are obviously low difference combinations; they tend to be stable and unified, and if not properly varied, they can of course be static.

In *direct complementary* schemes, complementary hues (for example, blue and orange) can be made to harmonize through corresponding adjustments in value and intensity. In *split complementary* systems, any hue is juxtaposed with the two hues which are on each side of its direct complement. Considered only as hue combinations, these two schemes are obviously high difference arrangements; they tend to be dynamic because of the breadth of their changes, and without adjustments to make them agree, they can appear chaotic.

Another conventional scheme, called *triadic*, has three hues which are equally separated on the color wheel (for example, green, orange, and violet). On a scale from high difference to low difference, triadic schemes are in between.

It would be wise to keep in mind that these particular schemes are terribly simplified notions. Indeed, there may be very few works of art (at least in terms of esthetic design) which would precisely fall within any of these categories. Further, an accomplished artist could conceivably achieve unity with variety through the use of any plan. Strict monochromatic systems are rare. Analogous systems with accents are seemingly easy to find, but there is not a single scheme (in terms of visual esthetic design) which is necessarily preferable to another.

Finally, there are books on graphic design which openly advise that the colors chosen for products or printed material should be simple and easy to name (for example, unmodified primary and secondary hues). In terms of marketing and the effective use of advertising, that advice would contradict what psychologists refer to as the *Zeigarnik effect*, a variation on that tendency of human perception which is most often called *closure*. Zeigarnik's principle simply predicts that things (such as color combinations) which are somewhat confusing, ambiguous, or disturbing will be more attended to and held in the memory longer than things which are simple and easy to name.

If Zeigarnik's principle works, advertisers might be wise to use ambiguous colors. In the same sense, for reasons of visual esthetic design, there are teachers of design who say that if the hues within a work can easily be named, the color scheme is probably lacking in richness.

The Primacy of Context

The principles used in art can almost always be applied throughout all of human life. This is especially true of simultaneous contrast, the significance and implications of which extend far beyond its uses in color or visual esthetic design. It has transformed our knowledge to the extent that it is one of a number of late nineteenth- and early twentieth-century concepts which are variously labeled *relativism, holism,* or *contextualism.*

ZEIGARNIK EFFECT   A principle of perception, proposed in 1927 by the Russian psychologist Bluma Zeigarnik, in which it is predicted that people will give attention to, and retain in the memory longer, things which are disturbing, unsolved, complex, or ambiguous. It is related to the common idea of *closure,* which the Gestalt psychologists proposed several years before.

All things are like the rainbow, for there is no phenomenon ''rainbow'' except where there is a certain relationship of sun, moisture in the atmosphere, and observer.

Alan W. Watts, *The Two Hands of God* (New York: Collier Books, 1969), p. 65.

Consider the philosophical implications when, as earlier noted, two samples of the same color are placed on different backgrounds. To greater or lesser degree, they appear to be two different colors. Which color is it? Is the "true" appearance of the color that which appears on the white background? On gray? On black? On green? Different color notation systems employ different backgrounds, and the answer seems to be that we cannot absolutely say what a color looks like except in relation to a specified surrounding.

A similar focus on contexts is characteristic of a large body of assumptions which are outside the field of art. In legal proceedings, defendants will plead that they are products of their environment. In ecological studies, we now know that the destruction of a rain forest will not just yield lumber—it will affect the plant and animal life, alter the culture of its human inhabitants, and even change the climate and atmospheric content of the earth itself. In psychology, we hear of family therapy, in which an entire family is treated rather than only the supposed patient. In physics, we are told of Heisenberg's principle of uncertainty, or the principle of complementarity, in which light may be defined as a wave or not a wave, depending on how we observe it.

The basic idea that all of these theories share is that *the character, appearance, or function of a thing is subject to modification when it is extracted from one environment and displaced to another,* or *that one cannot define a thing without describing its context.* This may be the most persuasive trait of the age in which we live.

Having now been introduced to color theory and terminology, along with the essence of context, you no doubt will realize that your success in using hues in visual esthetic design is still far from guaranteed. That will in part develop from examining works that others have done, and, most important, *repeatedly grappling with problems.*

In terms of visual esthetic design, there are general guidelines (the discrete use of accents, the counterbalanced play among the attributes of color) but there are no unqualified rules which govern the uses of color. That should not surprise you, since there are few immutable rules in virtually anything anyone does.

The so-called rules of color use are like the rudiments of chess. To be told that tints advance (or that certain hues are warm or that accents heighten hues) is somewhat like being taught that pawns can move one square ahead, that bishops move in diagonal paths, and so on. These rules, in and of themselves, do not teach us how to play.

As hard as chess can be, making complex works of art (devising esthetic arrangements) is considerably more difficult, in part because its rules are vague. The rules involved in playing chess are reasonably explicit. And yet it has been

CONTEXTUALISM The general idea that the nature of things can only be described or known in relation to (by comparing them with) other things or contexts. To follow, things may change in appearance when they are extracted from one environment and displaced to another (as in simultaneous contrast). The term means much the same as *holism* and *relativism*.

What is sauce for the goose may be sauce for the gander but it is not necessarily sauce for the chicken, the duck, the turkey, or the guinea hen.
Alice B. Toklas.

Many excellent cooks are spoiled by going into the arts.
Paul Gauguin.

FIGURE 2-16 Robert Cumming. *Watermelon/Bread.* 1970. Black and white photograph. Courtesy the artist. Beauty, Lautreamont once said, is the "chance encounter of a sewing machine and an umbrella on a dissecting table." In this photographic work, a slice of bread has been inexplicably embedded in a watermelon. It is a disturbing example of the tensions which result when a familiar object is taken out of context and displaced to a foreign ground.

said that a chess player, after ten moves, is faced with a choice of one move out of 165,518,829,100,544,000,000,000,000 possible actions, most of which would be unwise.

The rules of visual esthetic design are purposely tacit and almost always shifting; artists are commonly praised, in fact, for breaking expectations. Imagine how hard it is to choose when we have made ten "moves" while struggling with a work of art.

Chapter 3

Composition and Gestalt

Composing and Disposing

In music schools, there are courses in musical composition, the making of designs with sounds. If this were a book about music, I would discuss such things as rhythm, tempo, dynamics, timbre, and so on, which are often said to be the elements used in musical designs.

In language departments, there are courses in English composition, the making of designs with words. If this were a book on language, I would talk about such things as alliteration, assonance, rhyme, consonance, meter, and so on, since these are some of the ways by which written works are made to be esthetic.

Curiously, in schools of visual art, there is rarely a course entitled "composition." This is especially odd (in terms of visual esthetic design) since *composition* would seem to be a perfectly accurate word for what a lot of artists do. It is not often used now because, as words are known to do, it has acquired a bad reputation. Whatever its denotations, its connotations are repellent to many artists.

That the work of art has a formal structure of a rhythmical, even of a precisely geometrical kind, has for centuries been recognized by all but a few nihilists.

Sir Herbert Read, Preface to *Aspects of Form,* ed. L. L. Whyte (Bloomington: Indiana University Press, 1961).

FIGURE 3-1   William Bauman. *Untitled.* 1980. Gouache, 12″ × 15″. Courtesy the artist (student, University of Wisconsin—Milwaukee). The problem which this work resulted from required the depiction of a sheet of glass floating on a warped and patterned plane, with two objects on the glass. The surface is divided by coinciding diagonals, which serve as broken continuity lines.

COMPOSITION The construction of works of art (as well as other things in life) in which regard is given to the similarities and differences among their structural features (elements of design or grouping attributes), such as lines, textures, hues, values, intensities, shapes, and sizes. Composition is synonymous with patternmaking.

DISPOSITION The construction of works of art in which regard is given to their symbolic, representational, or pictorial significance. The term is not commonly used in this sense. It is synonymous with picture-making in the broadest meaning of that term. Works in which the disposition of subject matter has been disproportionately emphasized, with little or no regard for composition, are often disdained by artists as being merely illustrative.

I'll show you how to look at a picture, Cokey. Don't look at it. Feel it with your eye. . . . And first you feel the shapes in the flat—the patterns, like a carpet. . . . And then you feel it in the round. . . . Not as if it were a picture of anyone. But a coloured and raised map. You feel all the rounds, the smooths, the sharp edges, the flats and the hollows, the lights and shades, the cools and warms. The colours and textures. There's hundreds of little differences all fitting in together. . . .

Joyce Cary, *The Horse's Mouth* (New York: Time Incorporated, 1965), p. 145.

Words are symbols of ideas. By tracing the family history of a word, we can sometimes also trace the genealogy of an idea—its birth, its growth, its changes. The history of the word *composition,* however much it is not liked, may provide some insight into the history of the idea of design.

When something is composed, it is "put together." When something starts to decompose, it starts to rot or fall apart. The historical meanings of *composition* are somewhat vague (like our use of color terms), but as early as ancient Rome, its Latin equivalent (*compositio*) seems to have meant the way that parts of things are placed, their selection and arrangement.

Composition was at times distinguished from the act of disposition (not to be confused with the current use of that word). When one "disposed" an artwork, the subject matter was arranged so that it clearly pictured a certain object or event. When one "composed" an artwork, its structural features (colors, shapes, lines, textures) were arranged so that they exhibited some kind of order.

It may be a reasonable analogy to say that a mathematical "composition" would be an abstract equation like $x + y = z$. On the other hand, a mathematical "disposition" (of which there are an infinite number which have the same composition) would be a specific equation like $5 + 4 = 9$, or to specify further, that five apples plus four apples equals three-fourths of a dozen. Compositions are abstract relationships, which may carry or contain a large variety of dispositions, which are specific statements.

Patternmaking and Picture-making

As just stated, the word *composition* is begrudgingly used among visual artists. *Disposition* is hardly ever used today to talk about a work of art. Throughout history, there have been (and still are) people who believe that the primary function of art is the disposition of subject matter (*picture-making*). At the same time, there have been (and still are) people who say that the primary function of art is the composition of its structural features (*patternmaking*).

In terms of visual esthetic design, the composition of structural features (color, line, texture, shape, and so on) is of paramount importance. In terms of other intentions (for example, medical illustration, historical documentation, mechanical drawing, and so on), composition may be considerably less important.

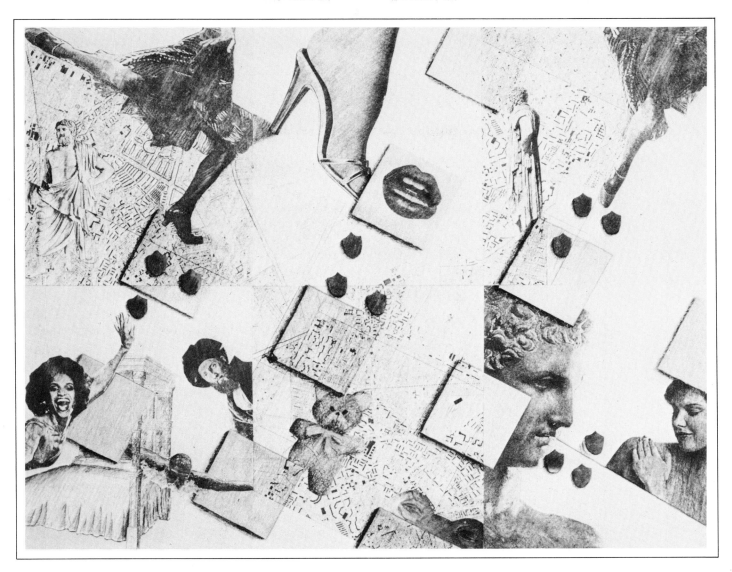

FIGURE 3-2 Dean Bressler. *Untitled.* 1980. Collage and mixed media, 12″ × 15″. Courtesy the artist (student, University of Wisconsin—Milwaukee). The total background is comprised of six square divisions, which are diagonally overlapped by nine smaller squares and four groups of smaller badgelike objects. The work's complexity results from the interweaving of those repetitive elements with the various figures, which alternately recede and advance.

An emphasis on composition in art was expressed by the French painter Maurice Denis, who said that "a painting—*before* being a war horse, a female nude, or whatever story—is essentially a flat surface covered with colors arranged in a certain order."

This does not imply that the design of "pictures" (the disposition of a work) is unimportant to artists. In one way or another, it has always been important to artists and probably always will be. In fact, when we discuss picture-making in the next chapter, I intend to show that it is even more important and more fascinating than most people realize. However, for the moment, it doesn't concern us.

Part and Whole Relationships

Maurice Denis' statement on war horses and nudes was first published in 1890. In the same year, Vincent van Gogh took his own life, William James published his *Principles of Psychology,* Paul Cézanne painted *The Cardplayers,* and James Frazer wrote *The Golden Bough.* In that same year in Germany, a psychologist named Christian von Ehrenfels published an essay entitled "On Gestalt Qualities" in which he used the term *Gestalt* in virtually the same sense that artists often use it now. In an approximate sense, it means "composition."

In vogue at the time of Ehrenfels' paper was a style of psychological research which, it may be fair to say, was chiefly interested in the "disposition" of things rather than in their "composition." Those who practiced this approach (usually called *atomism*) tended to interpret objects and events "from below." That is, they examined parts of things, with the assumption that larger wholes amounted to a sum of parts. Within this approach, the nature of things was absolute and not dependent on contexts.

Ehrenfels' essay questioned this belief. His ideas eventually led to a theory called *Gestalt,* which was contextual or holistic and interpreted things "from above." It might be said, in one sense, that Gestalt psychology was chiefly interested in the "composition" of things rather than in their "disposition." Indeed, the French refer to it as *la psychologie de la forme,* the psychology of form, and German-English dictionaries translate the word *Gestaltung* as arrangement or organization.

As Paul Weiss once said, atomism is like looking through the customary end of a telescope, thereby enlarging the details, whereas the holist looks

Under the microscope, even the clean edge of a knife becomes ragged.

Alan W. Watts, *The Two Hands of God* (New York: Collier Books, 1969), p. 2.

FIGURE 3-3 Paul Dickerson. *Untitled.* 1981. Gouache, 14″ × 17″. Courtesy the artist (student, University of Wisconsin—Milwaukee). The problem asked for hacksaw shapes, crosses, geometric shapes, and (alluding to Paul Klee) a line that is taking a walk, a walk for a walk's sake. Notice the figure-ground disruptions within the central parallelograms.

FIGURE 3-4 William Bauman. *Untitled.* 1980. Gouache, 14″ × 17″. Courtesy the artist (student, University of Wisconsin— Milwaukee). The central placement of the circle is counteracted by the off-center and downward position of the magnifying lens.

through the opposite end and sees the relations of things. Similarly, when artists examine the composition of a work of art, they sometimes squint (to blur their vision) in order to see larger relationships of color, line, texture, and other structural features rather than specific shapes.

To the Gestaltists, things are affected by where they are and by what surrounds them (as in simultaneous contrast), so that things are better described as "more than the sum of their parts." Obviously, there are advantages and disadvantages to both these approaches.

Contextualist notions were certainly not new in 1890, but Ehrenfels' paper was timely in helping to call attention to them. In his essay, Ehrenfels offered the simple example of a twelve-note melody played in two different keys. In either key, one cannot determine the melody by studying isolated notes, just as the letters *p, t, s,* and *o,* examined one at a time, do not foretell the "whole effect" of *pots* or *tops* or *stop* or *post*—or whatever one *opts* for.

Also, Ehrenfels noticed, although the version played in one key may not contain any of the same notes that exist in the other key, the melody is recognizable in both. Accordingly, the nature of wholes is not in their parts but rather in how they are "composed." The *Gestalt* (and this is the strict meaning of the term) is the ghostlike thirteenth feature—the structural aspect (the composition) or set of relationships ($x + y = z$) that can survive a change of parts.

Gestalt and Art

Ehrenfels lived until 1932. Except as a kind of hero, he seems to have played no role in the research of Max Wertheimer, who was offered research space and a tachistoscope (a device for projecting split-second images) at the Institute of Psychology in Frankfurt, Germany, in the fall of 1910. This was the real beginning of Gestalt psychology.

Wertheimer's suitcase contained a toy stroboscope (more commonly known as a strobe light). Using two of his students (Kurt Koffka and Wolfgang Köhler) as subjects, he began to experiment with *apparent movement,* the illusion that a number of lights, spaced apart and flashing one after another, appear to be one light that is moving.

Apparent movement is the basis for motion pictures, in which a number of pictures, shown one after another, appear to be one picture that is moving. It is also the basis for the illusory trail of blinking lights that seem to be circling the theater sign.

GESTALT A holistic style of psychology which originated in Germany prior to World War I. The Gestaltists (Wertheimer, Koffka, and Köhler) emphasized visual perception. They investigated figure and ground phenomena, developed the principles of perceptual organization (or the unit-forming factors, which are essentially the same as the principles of design), and stressed the contextual nature of things (the whole is greater than the sum of its parts). The German word *Gestalt* is most often said to mean "structure" or "arrangement."

. . . there is no thing, no event, save in relation to other things and events. . . .
Alan W. Watts, *The Two Hands of God,* p. 5.

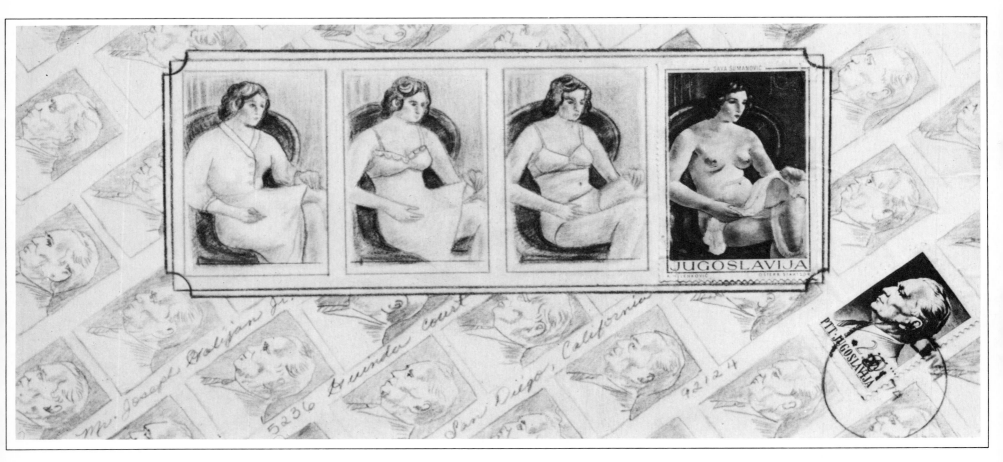

FIGURE 3-5 Sandra Greuel. *Untitled.* 1979. Collage and colored pencil, 9½″ × 4¼″. Courtesy the artist (student, University of Wisconsin—Milwaukee). This was one response to a problem similar to two-dimensional Problem Six, described in Chapter 6. The metamorphosis in the central panel is a clever application of apparent movement.

A Lot for the Money:
stories, poems, essays

Kenneth Lash

FIGURE 3-6 Connie Reed. Book jacket proposal. 1982. Courtesy the artist (student, University of Wisconsin—Milwaukee). This is a further use of visual metamorphosis.

UNIT-FORMING FACTORS Those tendencies of human perception by which we can anticipate which parts or features of a field will be seen as belonging together and which will be seen as belonging apart. The unit-forming factors are synonymous with the principles of perceptual organization, most of which can be reduced to the principle of similarity.

Recalling what Ehrenfels said about melodies, we can realize now that this illusion of movement is a "Gestalt quality"; it occurs because of the spacing and timing of the lights. If they are spaced too far apart or if the timing is delayed, the illusion will not occur.

The results of Wertheimer's experiments with apparent movement were published in 1912. They contain the basic ideas for his later writings on *unit-forming factors,* which are the very essence of the construction and interpretation of organized patterns—in visual esthetic design and throughout the rest of life.

In general, his writings ask one question: What characteristics of patterns make some features appear to belong together while others seem to fall apart? The answers he arrived at were called the *principles of perceptual organization,* or as we termed them previously, the unit-forming factors. It is precisely these findings which are the perceptual basis for visual esthetic design. They are the scientific base for the principles of design, since artists always use them (whether they know it or not) in composing works of art.

Figure and Ground

FIGURE AND GROUND The theory that any articulate visual field (a field in which a shape appears) must have at least two features: a salient portion called *figure* (which is what is focused on) and an indistinct portion called *ground* (behind or surrounding the figure). In a very general sense, all works of art are simply modulations of figure-ground relationships.

You may have already guessed that Wertheimer's unit-forming factors are used in a devious way in military camouflage. In fact, it was a rumor that one or more of the Gestalt psychologists may have assisted the German army in the development of military camouflage during World War I.

In camouflage, we are prevented from seeing a unit (the object that is hidden) because the camoufleur makes it blend with the features of what sur-

FIGURE 3-7 This drawing of a hypothetical ship is based on a dazzle camouflage scheme employed in World War I. Disruption of the figure prevented the enemy gunner from determining the exact speed and direction of the ship.

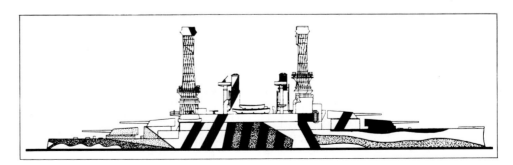

rounds it or makes it seem to break apart by using the tactic of dazzle. In camouflage, one way or another, we are prevented from seeing a *figure* (the thing) in the context of a *ground* (the background or surrounding).

A Danish psychologist, Edgar Rubin, who first wrote about figure and ground, referred to this relationship as *Dingcharakter und Stoffcharakter*, because a "thing" is only visible to the extent that it is dissimilar from a background of surrounding "stuff."

This seeming polarity of *similarity* (the parts of the figure must be of sufficient similarity so that they form a single thing) and *dissimilarity* (the figure must be of sufficient difference from its background so that it can be distinguished) is, as was implied before, a characteristic of *order*—any kind of order, whether sound in contrast to silence (as in music), inside in contrast to out (as in architecture), slow in contrast to fast, large to small, black to white, red to green, and so on.

When figures are not sufficiently different from their backgrounds, they blend with their surroundings and no "thing" is perceived. Or if the parts of a figure are not sufficiently similar, they will not group together and, again, no "thing" will form. These, as we have said before, are the conditions of anesthetic disorder.

ATTENTION In perception, a sorting or "filtering" process which allows us, at any one time, to focus on specific portions of our environment (figure) and to delay or neglect the remainder (ground). There are innumerable factors which determine if things will be attended to. Some of these include repetition, size, change, movement, intensity, novelty, and contrast, but all are dependent on context.

FIGURE 3-8 Malcolm Grear. Logo design for Mount Holyoke College, South Hadley, Massachusetts. 1967. Courtesy the designer. In reversible figure and ground, we can view the white area (H) as figure, or by a switch of attention, the black shape can be figure and the white can be ignored.

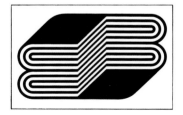

FIGURE 3-9 Malcolm Grear. Logo design for Brown University Press, Providence, Rhode Island. 1963. Courtesy the designer. Each side of this figure can be alternately viewed as advancing or receding.

FIGURE 3-10 In ambiguous figures, two pictures are contained within the same space.

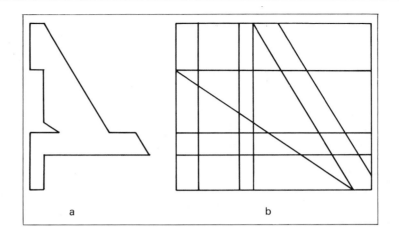

FIGURE 3-11 In embedded figure puzzles, we are asked to locate smaller shapes (a) which are concealed within larger complex units (b).

REVERSIBLE FIGURE AND GROUND Interlocked portions of a field which have certain features (equal size, equivalent novelty, and so on) which tend to make it likely that both can be focused upon equally. The result is a visual stalemate in which attention may suddenly switch, and what was initially figure may then be ignored as ground, and vice versa.

AMBIGUOUS FIGURES Various types of "puzzle pictures" in which two or more dispositional meanings are contained within one space. Most often, when viewed at a distance, these pictures appear to be one kind of object, but when examined more closely, they are comprised of other things, for example, a representation of a human face made by juxtaposing various fruits and vegetables. They are a type of visual pun.

EMBEDDED FIGURES Complex geometric shapes (commonly used in psychology tests) in which smaller shapes are hidden. The smaller shapes are hard to see because they make "good units" with (they are consistent with or similar to) the larger wholes in which they hide.

Over the years, Wertheimer and numerous others have described and listed all sorts of characteristics of figures and their backgrounds. Those most commonly talked about include *reversible figures and grounds, ambiguous figures,* and *embedded figures.* These are important to artists, although we need not list them all. In struggling with visual esthetic design, you will soon encounter most of them.

It is important to note that certain aspects of Rubin's ideas of figure and ground have not gone unquestioned, and there are those who disagree with some findings of Gestalt. However, most of Gestalt theory has been gradually absorbed by more recent styles of psychology, especially Wertheimer's principles of perceptual organization.

The Principle of Similarity

Wertheimer's principles of perceptual organization—his unit-forming factors—can be reduced to one general principle which should not surprise you. It is the *principle of similarity,* the theory that things which look alike will tend to be seen as belonging together, and things which look unlike will be seen as belonging apart. It is called by other names sometimes, such as *similarity grouping* or *perceptual grouping;* but in essence, it means, as Rudolf Arnheim (a student of Wertheimer and Koffka) said, "The relative degree of similarity in a given perceptual pattern makes for a corresponding degree of connection or fusion."

FIGURE 3-12 Paul Merklein. *Untitled*. 1982. Gouache, 9½″ × 14″. Courtesy the artist (student, University of Wisconsin—Milwaukee). This work is a solution to two-dimensional Problem Three, listed in Chapter 6. Notice the repeated use of reversible figure and ground.

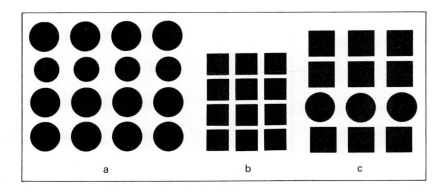

FIGURE 3-13   In similarity grouping, elements are seen as belonging together because of their similarity of size (a), position (b), shape (c), or any other visible attribute.

SIMILARITY GROUPING   The theory that things which look alike will tend to be seen as belonging together (which produces unity) and those which are dissimilar will be seen as belonging apart (which produces variety). However, no two things are inherently similar or different, since sorting depends on attention and which attributes are stressed.

PROXIMITY GROUPING   A special case of similarity grouping in which it is predicted that things which occur together in *space* will appear to belong together and those which are separated in space will appear to belong apart. It is grouping by similarity of location.

In terms of visual esthetic design, this principle is the most invaluable contribution of Gestalt psychology to the study of visual art. Studied with patience and care, it can allow insight into the interlacing of *unity* (brought about by similarity) and *variety* (brought about by difference) within a complex work of art.

Grouping by similarity (or the formation of units) can be based on as many comparisons as there are visible attributes of any shapes or objects. The obvious adhesives, of course, are those predominant attributes which books on art are likely to call "the elements of design"—hue, intensity, value, shape, texture, size, direction, location, speed, and so on. They are, as we mentioned before, what psychologists commonly call "grouping attributes."

To state it in a simpler way, the extent to which a work of art will be perceived as a unit (the extent to which it will be perceived as having *unity*) is directly dependent on the degree to which its various parts are similar in hue— or intensity or value or shape or texture or size. And the extent to which a work of art will be perceived as falling apart (the extent to which it will be perceived as having *variety*) is directly dependent on the degree to which its various parts are dissimilar in hue—or intensity or value or shape or texture or size.

Proximity and Contiguity Grouping

There are two cases of similarity grouping which often go by other names, *proximity* and *contiguity*.

It is anticipated by the *principle of proximity* that shapes or lines or objects will appear to belong together if they occur near to one another. This is grouping by similarity of location in space, and I know of no better example than an actual theatre board announcement, displayed outside a shopping mall, for a film version of *Romeo and Juliet*. The words on the board were grouped like this:

NO   ORDINARY

LOVE   STORY

so that I read the announcement as "no love, ordinary story," when it was intended to read "no ordinary love story." The spatial grouping of the words caused my confusion.

Even more commonly observed is the *principle of contiguity*, which predicts that things will tend to appear to belong together if they occur together in time. This is, obviously, grouping by similarity of occurrence in time. This seemingly simple assumption is basic to *cause and effect*. If I repeatedly punch a certain typewriter key and the letter *d* is typed, I am led to conclude that the latter is caused by the former. If that seems much too simple, consider the awesome complexity of searching for the cause or causes of cancer. What researchers essentially ask is this: What factors (smoking, stress, diet, environment, genetic factors, and so on) are repeatedly occurring together among the victims of cancer?

Contiguity grouping is equally essential to what is known as *behavioral conditioning*. Whenever Ivan Pavlov, the Russian psychologist, presented food to a dog, he also rang a bell. After a number of repetitions, the food was no longer presented, and yet the bell itself would "cause" the dog to salivate, *as if* the food were present.

One of Pavlov's most intriguing experiments was that in which a dog was rewarded whenever it was shown a circle, whereas the reward was withheld whenever it was shown an ellipse. Through a series of exposures, Pavlov gradually changed the circle's shape (making it more elliptical) and the shape of the ellipse (making it more circular). At about midpoint, when the two shapes were no longer distinguishable (and thus, the expectations of rewards and their withholding were also indistinguishable), the dog exhibited symptoms which resembled those of certain human neuroses.

This experiment (usually called *experimental neurosis*), along with subsequent research, may indicate that certain types of emotional illness can be brought about by repeated exposure to situations in which human beings can neither escape nor triumph. These may be (as some have said) *double-bind* encounters, in which one is "always in a bind," regardless of the choice one makes.

CONTIGUITY GROUPING A special case of similarity grouping in which it is predicted that things which occur together in *time* will appear to belong together and those which occur at different times will appear to belong apart. It is grouping by similarity of occurrence in time.

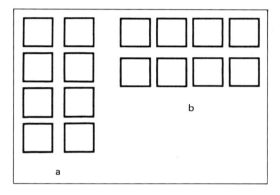

FIGURE 3-14 Because of proximity grouping (similarity of location), (a) is seen as vertical columns, and (b) is seen as lateral rows.

Behavioral psychology is the science of pulling habits out of rats.
Douglas Busch.

Double bind theory asserts that there is an experiential component in the determination or etiology of schizophrenic symptoms and related behavioral patterns, such as humor, art, poetry, etc. . . . Within its terms there is nothing to determine whether a given individual shall become a clown, a poet, a schizophrenic, or some combination of these.
Gregory Bateson, *Steps to an Ecology of Mind* (New York: Ballantine Books, 1972), p. 272.

FIGURE 3-15 Shirley Eliason Haupt. *Iowa/Black Field/Bernini.* 1971. Pencil and acrylic, 21″ × 21″. Courtesy the artist. In this remarkably sensitive use of figure-ground juxtaposition, the Bernini heads are hauntingly plaintive and fragile against the starkness of the ground.

The Complexity of Art

The operation of similarity grouping (the unit-forming factors) accounts for every "thing" we see. It is the basis for the grouping of stars into constellations, the perception of numbers in a test for color blindness, the recognition of the uniforms of two football teams, and the orchestration of intricate shapes within a complex work of art.

"The reason that iron filings placed in a magnetic field exhibit a pattern," as Christopher Alexander has said, "— or have form, as we say—is that the field they are in is not homogeneous (extreme similarity). If the world were totally regular and homogeneous, there would be no forces, and no forms. Everything would be amorphous." In physics, the term for states of extreme similarity or homogeneity is *entropy*.

If all we had to do in art was simply to make some parts appear to belong together and other parts appear to belong apart, visual esthetic design would be absurdly easy. Art is considerably harder than that.

The complexity of art is largely derived from the fact that parts may seem to connect on the basis of certain unit-forming factors (for example, similar hues) but be repelled by others (for example, different values). Further, most things are complex enough to exhibit a considerable number of features, all of which must be simultaneously accounted for.

As this is art's complexity, it is its source of intrigue, since it is this optical juggling act that yields the tenuous balance of unity with variety, on which esthetic works are based.

Visual Fragmentation

In terms of visual esthetic design, art is a delectable mixture of similarity and dissimilarity, order and disorder, unit-making and unit-breaking, consistency and surprise, repetition and variation, harmony and discord. Works of art make units, but they are fractured units or ones that are partially hidden. This factor is characteristic of visual esthetic design throughout the history of art, not just of so-called modern art, which, as Katherine Kuh has said, "has been characterized by shattered surfaces, broken color, segmented compositions, dissolving forms and shredded images."

The necessity of fragmentation (in whatever form it takes) is due to the fact that human beings experience art in much the same way that they experience

. . . the entropy principle defines order simply as an improbable arrangement of elements . . . and it calls disorder the dissolution of such an improbable arrangement.

Rudolf Arnheim, *Entropy and Art* (Berkeley: University of California Press, 1974), p. 15.

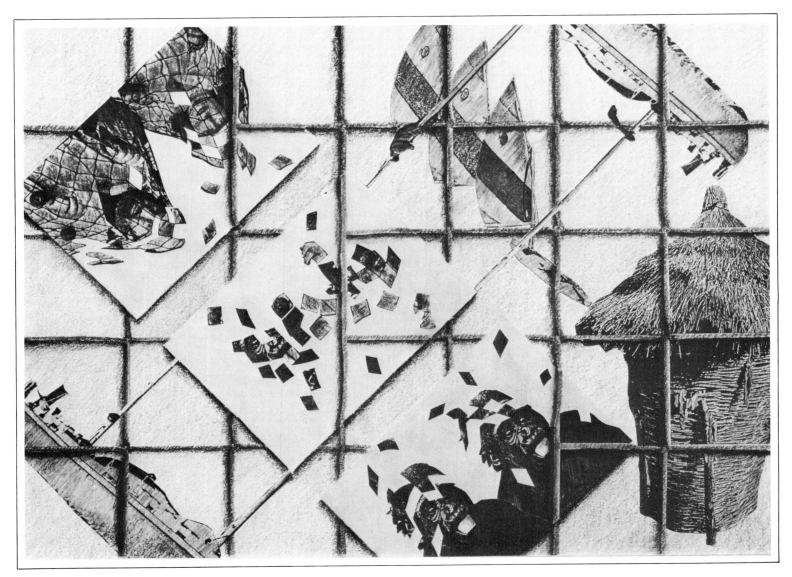

FIGURE 3-16 Dean Bressler. *Untitled.* 1980. Collage and colored pencil, 10″ × 14″. Courtesy the artist (student, University of Wisconsin—Milwaukee). This work resulted from a problem similar to two-dimensional Problem Five, listed in Chapter 6. Notice the fragmentation within the three diagonal rectangles and their interruption by the irregular background grid.

other things. Our feelings and comprehension of things are intensified by *participation*. As Zeigarnik's law predicts, we will give attention to, and hold in the memory longer, things which are disturbing, unsolved, puzzling, or ambiguous (the enigmatic smile of *Mona Lisa*, the Leaning Tower of Pisa, Gilbert Stuart's "unfinished" portrait of George Washington) because they are potential problems, which we are compelled to solve.

One would be mistaken then to think of works of art (as some people tend to do) as completed answers. The most compelling works of art are probably closer to riddles. They are flirtatious, incomplete, and always partially veiled. They tease us to complete them, to fill in the missing links. They are the "creations" of artists, but they must as well provide for the "re-creations" of the viewers.

. . . art is one of the most ambiguous of human activities, requiring a double consciousness—a sense of what is actual and a sense of what is feigned, a sense of participation and a sense of the fictitious. The only authentic artistic experience is perturbing. . . .

Wylie Sypher, jacket notes of *Art and Anarchy* by Edgar Wind (New York: Vintage Books. 1969).

FIGURE 3-17 Dick Evans. *Delton Dusk.* 1979. Porcelain, 10″ × 16″ × 4″. Collection of Jeff and Susan Becherer. Courtesy the artist. By slicing the original form and spacing the segments apart, the artist assured the closure process when the sculpture is perceived.

FIGURE 3-18   William Bauman. *Untitled*. 1980. Gouache, 6″ × 15″. Courtesy the artist (student, University of Wisconsin—Milwaukee). This work was an answer to an "absurd sentence" problem which was similar to two-dimensional Problem Four, discussed in Chapter 6. This same work was then used to develop Problem Two.

The task of an artist is probably akin to that of a maker of crossword puzzles. The artist must provide the clues but not the answers.

Each time we solve a puzzle, we tend to become increasingly skilled at solving riddles of that sort. We run the risk of being bored, of no longer facing a challenge, of losing our base for involvement unless subsequent puzzles are gradually made to be harder—by the withholding of previous clues, by playing within time constraints, by facing a tougher opponent, and so on.

In much the same way, the history of styles of art is an evolution of increasingly difficult puzzles. When a style of art is born, it is confusing and obtuse. Every significant movement in art is initially condemned. With time and repeated encounters, the audience adopts the game, providing the viewers are willing to play. But then again, as skills increase, the nature of the game must change, and yet another style is born. More difficult methods of teasing evolve. Fewer clues are given away. Increasingly more information is hidden or offered in a cryptic way.

As Arthur Koestler (who said all this years ago) put it, "symmetry and asymmetry, closure and gap, continuity and contrast" must intermix in works of art, and "the surest symptom of decadent art is that it leaves nothing to the imagination . . . there is no veiled promise, no mystery, nothing to divine."

Art, as the painter Magritte once said, is "innocent mystification." He enshrouded human heads by floating apples in front of their eyes.

A picture is something which requires as much knavery, trickery, and deceit as the perpetration of a crime. Paint falsely, and then add the accent of nature.

Edgar Degas, quoted in Robert Goldwater and Marco Treves, eds., *Artists on Art* (New York: Pantheon Books, 1945), p. 308.

Closure

When Koestler says "closure and gap," he is referring to a principle of Gestalt psychology which is essentially the same as audience involvement. The artist creates clues and gaps. The primary task of the viewer is to re-create those parts which might best resolve the gaps. The closure principle predicts that clues and hints will cause the mind to try to solve the unresolved, to finish what is not complete, to see as continuous units things which have been broken or which are in part concealed.

Throughout the history of art, countless methods have evolved to withhold information, to make sure that gaps exist. Thus, whatever else it did, linear perspective (invented in the Renaissance) left out information which earlier art had provided. And whatever else it did, chiaroscuro (the use of shading and highlights to depict the roundness of objects) enshrouded shapes in shadows and teased with lost-and-found contour.

CLOSURE   A unit-forming factor or principle of perceptual organization in which it is predicted that patterns which are incomplete will tend to be completed (by the viewer) in the process of being perceived.

LOST-AND-FOUND CONTOUR   The juxtaposition of extremely lightened tints with extremely darkened shades, so that the lightened parts are clear and the darkened parts are "lost." The contrast of the lighted "clues" with the blurred or obscured "gaps" insures that closure will occur. It is essentially the same as *chiaroscuro* (light-dark, clear-obscure), the use of pronounced shadows, which came into common use in the sixteenth and seventeenth centuries.

FIGURE 3-19 These are various examples of incomplete figures which, because of closure, appear as continuous circles in the process of being perceived.

FIGURE 3-20. Lippincott and Margulies, Inc., New York. Logo for Eaton Corporation, Cleveland, Ohio. 1971. Courtesy Eaton Corporation. In this elegant and inventive use of lost-and-found contour, the edges of the white letters are alternately omitted and clearly described.

FIGURE 3-21 Malcolm Grear. Logo design for Color Concentrate Corporation, Woonsocket, Rhode Island. 1962. Courtesy the designer. The ghostlike white triangle in the center of the logo is a cognitive contour as well as an example of reversible figure and ground.

FIGURE 3-22 *Coincident disruptive pattern* is a zoological term for animal forms in which the surface pattern on one part of the body appears to continue onto another separate part. The white elongated crescent shape on this butterfly appears to continue onto all four wings.

IMPLIED LINE Especially in drawing, the linear equivalent of lost-and-found contour. The pressure of the hand is changed so that the line changes from thick to thin, dark to light, and clear to faint. The act of closure is insured by the skillful alternation of clarity (found) and obscurity (lost).

Closure is one reason why artists who draw figures often modulate the lines which border the shapes they are drawing. Lines may move from thick to thin. They may even disappear. These are called *implied lines,* and artists who use them are careful to record those points where essential changes exist (where the ear and jaw connect, the tip of the elbow, the termination of the mouth) so that the viewer can connect the dots or clues and bridge the gaps.

Implied line and lost-and-found contour are two fairly common ways by which artists insure gaps (lost) within a range of careful clues (found). There is a host of other means (some of which are picture clues, some of which are pattern hints), which go by all sorts of names, including *cognitive contours, grid systems,* and *coincident disruptive patterns.* These will be discussed again, in the next chapter, where they are referred to as *broken continuity clues.* All we need to know right now is that techniques of this sort trigger participation—they activate the viewer's mind, causing re-creation.

Finally, trained or untrained, the eye will tend to fill the gaps in the simplest possible way. The Gestaltists referred to this as the *principle of continuity* (or, sometimes, as *simple form*). In completing broken forms, we tend to take the shortest path between two clues or given points, the most parsimonious route.

Thus, when closure does not work (in drawing, in design, in love affairs), the invitation is refused or a wrong response results for one of two evident reasons: The clues which have been offered are of insufficient number, so that there is too much fragmentation to enable the viewer to build an intelligible unit; or the nature and placement of clues are such that they will foster units distinctly different from those which the artist intended. Obviously, crossword puzzles can fail for the same two reasons.

The principle of closure (that we tend to fill in gaps) and Zeigarnik's principle (that unclosed forms will vex the mind) are essentially the same. These two principles suggest that if we want to produce compelling art, we should never spell things out, that lasting art is always perturbing or puzzling.

The Validity of Design

It would be wise to wonder if theories of composition in visual esthetic design amount to so much nonsense. There are surely those who think that the unit-forming factors of Gestalt psychology (which are essential to design) are not mental tendencies which all human beings share. These principles are, they might contend, the conspiratorial fictions of snobbish "modern artists," who spread the word through schools of art so that their gullible students will continue to believe (as, indeed, one sometimes hears) that the emperor's clothing is there when in fact he is naked.

Curiously enough, camouflage is one response to questions of this sort. The effectiveness of camouflage among human beings has been repeatedly proven in war. Camouflage is dependent on the unit-forming factors (the princi-

COGNITIVE CONTOUR A type of reversible figure and ground in which ghostlike floating shapes are implied by irregular notches or gaps in the figures of a field. Also called *subjective contour.*

GRID SYSTEMS Straight-line axes or subdivisions which interrupt or coincide with the features of a work (lines, shapes, textures) so that a framework is implied. These "informal subdivisions" (as they are sometimes referred to) may be few or many, and they may be horizontal, vertical, or diagonal.

COINCIDENT DISRUPTIVE PATTERNS A term employed by Hugh B. Cott, the British zoologist, to refer to lines or shapes which are both interrupted and continuous. Often they resemble the shifts or "faults" (breaks in the continuity) in the pattern of a rock. The same effect can be observed between the upper and lower wings of some butterflies and moths.

Painting is a blind man's profession. He paints not what he sees, but what he feels, what he tells himself about what he has seen.

Pablo Picasso (reported by Jean Cocteau).

FIGURE 3-23 Shirley Eliason Haupt. *Homage to Dietrich Bonhoeffer (1906–1945)*. 1967. Charcoal, 19″ × 25″. Collection of Jean Valentine. Courtesy the artist. There is a delicate use of implied line throughout much of this work, as each line moves from thick to thin. Because of its juxtaposition of radically differing halves, it is a clear example of asymmetrical balance.

ples of perceptual organization) of Gestalt psychology. If, through similarity grouping, we can predictably deceive the eyes of soldiers from all over the world (without their being trained to see), surely we can then believe that these same grouping factors can achieve the same result when they are used in works of art.

As artists have often realized (some have taught and practiced it), the tools and procedures of camouflage are virtually identical to those of visual esthetic design. The end results, however, are not the same. Effective camouflage depends on disorder; it distracts and hides. Art must hide to some extent, not with the aim of concealing the thing, but as Arthur Koestler says, of "making it more luminous by compelling the recipient to work it out by himself—to re-create it."

Successful camouflage conceals. The aim of art is to *reveal*—through pictures (disposition) and through patterns (composition).

Chapter 4

Pictures and Patterns

The Priority of Patterns

In the second half of the sixteenth century (during the Inquisition), an Italian painter named Paolo Caliari was hired by the Roman Catholic church to paint the final supper of Christ and his disciples.

Having completed the painting, the artist was summoned before the tribunal of the Holy Office in 1573. There he was accused of adding impertinent details to the scene he had painted. Not only had he depicted Christ and the Apostles, his painting also included two guards dressed in German clothes, a parrot, a dwarf, a dog, and a man with a bleeding nose.

What did he intend by this? Did he insert such scurrilous details, the tribunal asked, for the purpose of "mocking, abusing, and ridiculing the things of the Holy Catholic Church, in order to teach the false doctrine to the illiterate and ignorant?"

The painter replied calmly (he may have been promised protection by higher authorities) that these unusual details were not only proper but necessary because the composition *demanded* that something be put in those spaces. "I was

If your man says of some picture, "Yes, but what does it mean?" ask him, and keep on asking him, what his carpet means, or the circular patterns on his rubber shoe-soles. Make him lift up his foot to look at them.

Stephen Potter, *The Complete Upmanship* (New York: New American Library, 1978), p. 202.

FIGURE 4-1   Chris Van Allsburg. *The Carpet Theft*. 1979. Conté on paper, 20″ × 28″. Collection of Barnet Fain. Courtesy the artist and Allan Stone Gallery, New York. This fascinating drawing by an accomplished children's book illustrator makes effectively teasing use of a kind of narrative closure. One cannot confront the work without being puzzled by who is stealing the carpet and why.

What garlic is to salad, insanity is to art.
Augustus Saint-Gaudens.

VISUAL WEIGHT   The extent to which any features in a work are likely to be given weight, attended to or focused on. *Weight* is used as a metaphor here, and visual weight is not the same as physical heaviness or poundage, just as we do not imply actual gravitational pull when we speak of the gravity of a situation. In visual esthetic design, the determinants of weight would appear to be the same as the determinants of attention—size, position, value, intensity, change, movement, novelty, contrast, and so on.

VISUAL BALANCE   The somewhat vague sensation of equilibrium, equity, or just proportion in a work. It seems to be dependent on the extent to which any one predominant part is countervailed or offset by other parts with equal weight. In works which are disproportionate or imbalanced (much as in mental imbalance), a single part has too much weight (which destroys the effect of the whole) or all parts have equal weight (which usurps the strength of the parts).

commissioned," he said, "to adorn the picture as I judged best, and it is large, and had room for many figures, as it seemed to me."

Further, he explained, the disposition of the work (the selection and placement of subject matter) was appropriate also, since it would be "realistic" to assume that characters of this sort (the German guards, the dog, the dwarf) would have been at Simon's house on the night that Christ was there. (One of the Apostles is even depicted as cleaning his teeth.)

Caliari pleaded that (like Michelangelo before him) he should not be told how to arrange his paintings, because that is solely determined by the compositional and dispositional requirements of the work itself—not by the tribunal's restrictions. "We painters," he entreated, "take the same liberties that poets, comics and madmen take."

Under threat of punishment, the artist was ordered to alter the work. He did, but not completely. The bloody nose was taken out, but all the other parts remain. Caliari survived; he is more commonly known as the painter Veronese, and the painting is now called *Supper in the House of Levi* (not the house of Simon), having been retitled so that it is no longer a depiction of the Last Supper.

Balance and Visual Weight

Almost exactly one hundred years before Veronese's trial, an Austrian painter (his name has since been lost) produced a picture of *Saint Michael Weighing Souls*. In a roughly symmetrical pattern, St. Michael is shown in the center, with an angel on each side, as he weighs the spiritual goodness of figures in a balance scale.

In the right pan of the scale, four large dark devils sit beside two millstones. In the left pan, one small light-skinned Christian figure kneels in prayer. The scale is tipped in the Christian's direction. Obviously, the pictorial message (the dispositional meaning) is that spiritual goodness far outweighs the devils' sins.

In terms of theology, all this is fine, and the painter might have stopped right there—but he encountered a terrible problem. That problem derives from the fact that structural features of works of art (whatever their disposition) convey sensations of *visual weight*.

More specifically, large shapes are generally perceived as "heavier" than small shapes; that is, we give more weight to them, or see them as more pon-

FIGURE 4-2 Austrian (artist unknown). *St. Michael Weighing Souls.* c. 1470–1480. Tempera on panel, $36\frac{3}{4}'' \times 30\frac{1}{2}''$. Collection of Allen Memorial Art Museum, Oberlin College, Oberlin, Ohio. R. T. Miller, Jr., Fund, 43.113.

SYMMETRICAL BALANCE An equitable distribution of visual weight achieved by juxtaposing highly similar lateral halves. Strict applications of bilateral symmetry (mirror-image halves) and radial symmetry (kaleidoscopic repetitions around a central focal point) are extremely rare in visual esthetic design, though common in religious art. When artists employ formal symmetry, they must in some way "break" it (hence, the term *broken symmetry*) to avoid monotony.

ASYMMETRICAL BALANCE A "high difference" method of distributing visual weight, in which two remarkably different halves are directly juxtaposed—black against white, a hue against its complementary hue, filled space against empty space, and so on.

derous, since visual weight is not the same as literal weight as measured in pounds. In the same sense, shapes of darker value appear to be heavier than shapes of light value. A greater number of shapes will generally tend to appear heavier than will a lesser number, and so on. By juggling these and other traits, artists can make parts of works appear to call for equal weight—or, as is commonly said, to have *visual balance*.

This fifteenth-century painter encountered a curious problem because the dispositional message of his work (its *pictorial meaning*) was contradicted by the compositional structure (its *pattern meaning*). The picture was intended to say that one virtuous figure carries more weight than four sinful figures and two millstones. But all the structural characteristics of visual weight (value, number, and size) had been given to the devils—they were darker in value, considerably greater in number, and occupied a larger space. Accordingly, despite how the scale was tipped, the devils had more "ponderousness"—that is, they were more "weighty"—than the tiny praying man.

FIGURE 4-3 The human face is frequently cited as an example of bilateral symmetry, yet everyone's face, to some extent, is also asymmetrical. Of these three photographs, the one in the center is a normal image. By flipping the negative to make a reversed print, we can combine identical halves to make two strange symmetrical pairs. Photograph by Ruth Kao.

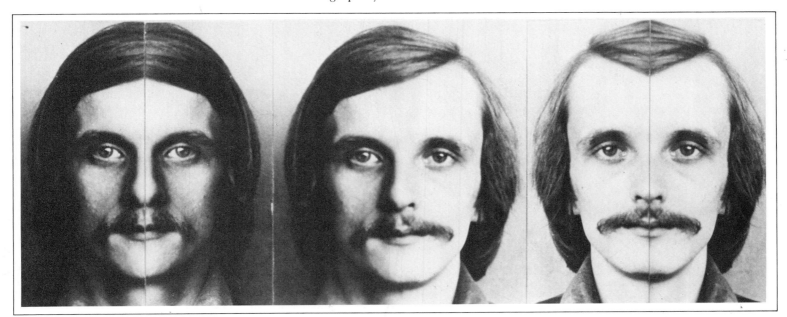

How was the problem resolved? As Rudolf Arnheim pointed out, in the lower center of the painting (directly beneath the Christian) the painter inserted an odd and rather irrelevant shape (it seems to be a floating scroll) which equals the weight of the devils. Now, in terms of both picture and pattern, the Christian's side has more weight than the side of the devils.

Broken Continuity Clues

There is another peculiar aspect of this strange shape beneath the Christian. It is curved and carefully placed in such a way that it appears to connect with, to be one of, to "belong to" (by similarities of value, shape, and placement) a series of three or four dark background areas directly to its right and left (these outline the angels' robes).

In fact, should you squint your eyes (or view it from a distance), you might at first mistake it for one of those shapes; and you might for a moment believe that part of an arc or circular curve is cutting across the background in the lower quarter of the work. Indeed, it may remind you of "broken circle" diagrams used as examples of closure and gap. It may also make you think of implied lines, lost-and-found contours, cognitive contours, coincident disruptive patterns, and so on.

This teasingly "there-but-not-there" curve (found, then lost, then found again) is one of the guises of closure and gap, which we discussed in Chapter 3. It is a widely used device for building compositions which are at the same time *continuous* (for the purposes of unity) and *discontinuous* (for the purposes of variety and involvement).

It cannot hurt to say again that devices of this kind are found in works of visual art throughout the entirety of art history. They are even more commonly used in the layout of publications (they exist throughout this book), or even in a page of type, since paragraph indentations imply a broken upright line, which is of course the "margin." They occur so often in graphic design, where they are usually called *grid systems*, that entire books have been written about how to use them.

These "there-but-not-there" ghostlike clues need not be made with shapes or lines. They can as well result from corresponding broken hues, intensities, values, textures, and so on—in fact, any visual traits can be used to imply forms. I have decided to call them *broken continuity clues*. They are never called that

INFORMAL BALANCE   A casual, unpredictable distribution of visual weight which does not use opposing halves. It is usually devised by intuition rather than analysis, and in visual esthetic design, it may be used more frequently than symmetrical and asymmetrical balancing schemes.

A portrait is a picture in which there is something wrong with the mouth.
Eugene Speicher.

BROKEN CONTINUITY CLUES   In patternmaking and picture-making, features which are simultaneously continuous and interrupted. Continuities are clues, whereas interruptions provide gaps. Together, they cause closure. There are innumerable kinds of these, of which a few include lost-and-found contours, implied lines, cognitive contours, grid systems, coincident disruptive patterns, overlapping, and all perspective systems.

PRINCIPLE OF CONTINUATION A unit-forming factor or principle of perceptual organization in which it is predicted that the gaps in unclosed forms will be completed (when perceived) along the simplest, most effortless path. It is related to (and perhaps synonymous with) the principle of simple form.

(indeed, they are rarely discussed), but it may be a usable coinage since the term itself implies the *principle of continuation*, which as we discussed before, predicts that we will fill in gaps in the most effortless manner—that closure will follow the easiest path.

Again, the essential thing to know is that clues like this are used to hold a work together by virtue of our tendency toward closure and continuation, and

FIGURE 4-4 Joe Sutter. Poster design for Fine Arts Theater, University of Wisconsin—Milwaukee. 1981. As is evident in this poster and the accompanying diagram, it was precisely organized so that most edges coincide with an implied system of horizontal and diagonal axes.

their interruptions (their fragmentations or their gaps) compel us to participate. Further, the "broken" aspect insures *variety* or difference (that is, unit-breaking), and the "continuity" aspect insures *unity* or similarity (that is, unit-making).

Compositional Resemblances

When we look at artworks with broken continuity clues in mind, some rather surprising structural or compositional resemblances become evident between works with radically different subject matter. Works of rather recent years (which may not have obvious "pictures") may begin to look a lot like works of much earlier periods of history. Or contemporaneous works, depicting different subject matter in differing styles, made by different artists in different countries, even different cultures, may seem to have nearly the same composition.

For example, there is, as everyone knows, a famous painting by James McNeill Whistler which depicts his mother. Whistler was primarily concerned with visual esthetic design, with the structural features of artworks. His painting is *not* entitled *Whistler's Mother,* although everyone calls it that. It is entitled *Arrangement in Gray and Black No. 1: The Artist's Mother.*

If you examine that painting in search of broken continuity clues, you can find ample evidence of Whistler's use of this device.

Art is not an imitation of life. One of the damned things is enough.

Virginia Woolf.

FIGURE 4-6 Diagram based on a portrait by Gustav Klimt, entitled *Fritza Riedler.* There is a surprising compositional resemblance between this work and Whistler's portrait of his mother. Notice the broken continuity line which undercuts the subject's chin.

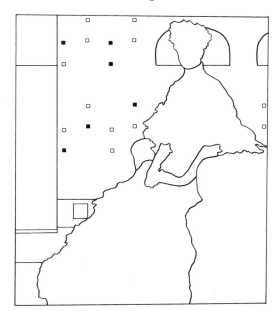

FIGURE 4-5 Diagram based on *Arrangement in Gray and Black No. 1* by James Abbott McNeill Whistler, completed in 1871–1872. Notice the broken continuity line that coincides with the bottom edges of the two picture frames and the tip of the figure's nose.

Whistler's title, Arrangement in Gray and Black No. 1, *has ironically been personalized into* Whistler's Mother—*the public was not ready for "arrangements."*

Marshall McLuhan and Harley Parker, *Through the Vanishing Point* (New York: Harper and Row, 1969), p. 169.

Thus, if you place a ruler or straightedge on a reproduction of the painting so that the edge of the ruler coincides with the bottom edge of the central picture frame within the work, you may be surprised. There is an implied line (or a broken continuity line) which underlies that picture frame, intersects the very tip of the nose of Whistler's mother, and is then picked up on the right side by the bottom of a second picture frame. The use of the nose is ingenious, since its tip is a focal point where a sudden change of direction occurs, just like the tip of the elbow which (as mentioned in Chapter 3) figure artists sometimes stress.

Having looked at Whistler's painting, you might then examine a considerably different portrait by the Viennese artist Gustav Klimt, entitled *Fritza Riedler.* By aligning a straightedge with the bottom of the seemingly meaningless shape on the upper right side of the work (compare that shape with the fragment of a frame on the right of Whistler's painting), you can follow another broken continuity line which leads to the left, to the shape behind the subject's head, to tiny squares, and then to the large rectangular shape in the upper left corner. In terms of this aspect and a number of other divisions, the composition of Klimt's painting begins to look remarkably like the structure of Whistler's work.

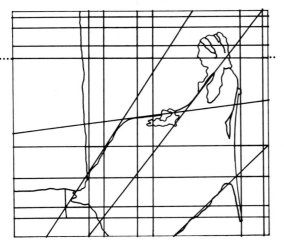

FIGURE 4-7 As this diagram demonstrates, most of the structural axes in Whistler's *Arrangement in Gray and Black* are horizontal and vertical, with a few diagonal accents.

The Meaning of Structural Features

It is essential to remember that we have examined only one structural feature of these works, their use of broken continuity lines. There are innumerable other traits (value, shape, hue, and so on) which contribute just as much in terms of both patterns and pictures.

For example, if Whistler's painting is further dissected to mark out other structural lines, it becomes apparent that it consists of a predominance of horizontal and vertical axes (broken continuity lines), with a few diagonal accents.

We often say that pictures are "representations," but lawyers "represent" their clients, and flags (or even diplomats) can "represent" a government. If a representation, or "picture," can be broadly thought of as any kind of conveyance or symbolization of feelings, ideas, or things, we can begin to realize how esthetically structured arrangements (compositions) can operate in tandem with the eloquent uses of pictures (dispositions).

In this sense, Whistler's painting can be said to picture, or represent, a certain range of meanings precisely because (among other factors) he has chosen to compose with predominant horizontals and verticals and with diagonal accents. For whatever biological reason (probably related to our sense of gravity, balance, and equilibrium), artists have always noticed that *horizontal* structures (somehow) convey feelings of restfulness, nonmovement, and stability. *Vertical* structures convey a feeling of erect but directed alertness; and *diagonal* structures convey feelings of tension, instability, and ambiguity.

In this sense, we could say that Whistler was addressing a problem very similar to that which the fifteenth-century Austrian painter dealt with when he made both the compositional and dispositional features of his work proclaim that "the Christian's side weighs more."

Whistler's statement is not theology, of course. It is an intricate comment on (true or false, we do not know) a somber bouquet of emotions about the person who gave birth to him. To reduce the painting's "picture" to the point of inanity, it "means" in an awesomely complex way, "This woman possesses a distant and somber dignity."

Now, it is entirely possible that Whistler's actual mother was not like this at all (she may have been a raving idiot), and this is a wishful picture. But, you must remember, artists are not inventors of mothers or war horses or nudes. They are inventors of works of art—and the requirements and characteristics of the one are vastly different from the requirements and characteristics of the other. This is what Veronese meant when he insisted that the requirements and characteristics of his painting could not be decided by the tribunal's conception of the requirements and characteristics of the Last Supper.

We could continue to explain how all sorts of other structural (or compositional) features within Whistler's painting contribute to its "picture." That in itself could fill a book.

However, it may be enough to note that the painting's color consists of predominant darker hues (tones and shades), with lighter values as accents. The low contrast and the optical recession of the predominant colors, along with their coolness, are evocative parallels to emotional distance, affective reserve, and comparable personality traits of a stable but nondemonstrative person. From this painting, we would not expect this dignified person to laugh or shout. She may not even face us. Notice also that the lines and shapes within the work do not change suddenly or unpredictably, and most, in fact, are rather straight. Further, the body and the head are shown in an unambiguous profile, with little or no promise of change or double meaning. There is a degree of severity here, perhaps even coldness.

In general, structural features (as Whistler knew) which are dark, cool, horizontal, predictably spaced, smooth, symmetrical, recessive, and unam-

The air that we see in the paintings of the old masters is never the air that we breathe.
Edgar Degas.

The map is not the territory.
Alfred Korzybski.

Einstein's space is no closer to reality than Van Gogh's sky.
Arthur Koestler, *The Act of Creation* (New York: Macmillan, 1964), p. 252.

FIGURE 4-8 Susan Miles. *When We Are Dancing.* 1980. Watercolor 15 ″ × 22″. Courtesy the artist. Two parallel broken continuity lines run across this painting of a dance studio interior with two mirrors on the wall. Added tension occurs because the room's perspective implies a three-dimensional space which is contradicted by the flat plane in the mirrors.

FIGURE 4-9 Orazio Fumagalli. *Figure Fragment No. 1.* 1978. Plaster-fabric shell sculpture, 32″ × 43″. Courtesy the artist. Much of the power of this work is due to its daring omissions—the interruption of the arms, the extraction of the face. It is an apt example of the use of clues and gaps, of putting in and leaving out.

No language, no sign system . . . is isomorphic with the world, or can be. No sign system has the same structure as the world.

Morse Peckham, *Man's Rage for Chaos* (New York: Schocken Books, 1967), p. 92.

biguous tend to depict *stability*, or a kind of lack of engagement. They are allied to a great extent with sensations of unity.

Structural features which are light, warm, diagonal, unpredictably spaced, rough, asymmetrical, advancing, and ambiguous tend to depict *instability*, that is, engagement and change. They are allied to a great extent with sensations of variety. It seems reasonable that in most artworks there is a predominance of one or the other extreme, although the two are also mixed.

Now, to recall Chapter 2, it may be clearer why the sale of cigarettes is so directly dependent on the color of their cartons, the typeface, and the brand name. *We probably tend to buy those things which look and feel like us.* We buy "pictures" of ourselves, whether cool, tough, or sophisticated.

Problems of Representation

All this may surprise you if you grew up (as I did) thinking and believing that works of art are simply "painted photographs," the quality of which is judged by the extent to which they look like photographs of actual things. Fortunately or unfortunately, life is not so simple.

In fact, when you think about *likeness* (and very few people seem to), the making and viewing of works of art take on a baffling complexity, which could easily occupy the remainder of our lives. If only it were as simple as Leonardo must have thought when he made a note in his journal, "That painting is most praiseworthy which is most like the thing represented."

What we regard as the most realistic pictures are merely pictures of the sort that most of us, unfortunately, are brought up on. An African or a Japanese would make a quite different choice when asked to select the pictures that most clearly depict what he sees.

Nelson Goodman, "The Way the World Is," in *Review of Metaphysics*, September 1960, p. 52.

If we follow Leonardo's rule, we immediately run into immense difficulties. To determine if an artwork is most like the thing it represents, we must know at least two things: What is the nature of the thing represented? And how can we make an artwork which is most like that thing?

The first problem we encounter (as we found in simultaneous contrast) is that the contextual modification of things makes it virtually impossible to say what a thing is like. If we should define a thing, we must denote the context (the situation) and the manner of viewing in terms of which it is defined. Within other contexts, or viewed through other means of sight, the features of the thing will change.

This particular problem has intensified astoundingly in the past few hundred years, with the invention of tools and methods for viewing which have extended the range of what a thing is "like." The more familiar now include X-

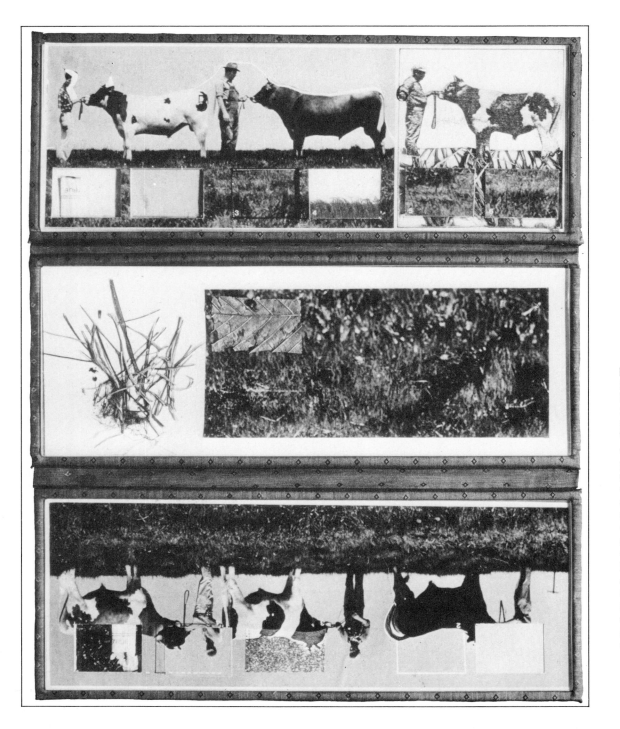

FIGURE 4-10 Kathryn M. Kreige. *Cow Gameboard.* 1980. Mixed media construction, $10\frac{1}{2}''$ × $13\frac{1}{2}''$. Courtesy the artist (student, University of Wisconsin—Milwaukee). This work was an answer to a problem, similar to that described in Chapter 7, in which the artist was asked to develop the gameboard, box, and pieces for a game for which the rules are lost. It combines photographic collage with actual samples of grass, leaves, and cigarette butts, covered by plexiglas and trimmed with a decorative fabric. Notice the playful changes as the rows of rectangles intersect the rows of cows.

rays, microphotography, thermograms, laser holography, infrared devices, color coding, time-lapse photography, gamma ray images, sonography, stroboscopic photography, and so on. In combination with our increased awareness of the importance of context, these new modes of viewing have brought us to the point at which, as Siegfried Kracauer says, *"Not one single object has retained a fixed, definitely recognizable appearance."*

Perhaps you think this assertion begs the point, but even if we do succeed in defining the nature of the thing represented, we are left with the second dilemma: How shall we make an artwork which is most like the thing represented?

If we make an artwork which is entirely (in all respects) like the thing represented, we will not end up with an artwork. We will end up with the thing itself, or at least a clone of it. But artists, as we said before, are not inventors of things that are represented; they are inventors of *representations* of things.

The painter René Magritte referred to precisely this problem when he made a painting of a pipe and then wrote beneath it, *Ceci n'est pas une pipe* ("This is not a pipe"). And, of course, it's *not* a pipe. It is instead a painting, and the requirements and characteristics of pipes are not those of paintings.

In terms of representing life (whether through patterns or "pictures" or both), the power of art is twofold: in its similarity to the thing represented and in its *difference*. The fact that it differs from "real things" is precisely why it's *art*. It is artifice or pretense, which is not the same as life.

It must follow then that works of art are like the thing represented in terms of some features and unlike the thing represented in terms of other features. But now another problem appears: How shall we determine which features of the thing represented shall be included in the artwork and which features shall be left out?

Some people would reply that obviously we should include those features of the thing that will provide us with the most "realistic" picture. But what is "realism" if not the inclusion of features? And so again, we have to ask: What features should be emphasized to make a work "realistic"?

Should it be the "realism" of a photograph? But *which* photograph? Taken with what camera? With what lens? Under what conditions of lighting? With what kind of film? With what film speed? With what aperture setting, what focus, what shutter speed? Printed on what paper? Developed according to what chemical procedure?

The "distortion" of the photograph is comparable to the distortion of new or unfamiliar styles of painting.

Nelson Goodman, "The Way the World Is," p. 52.

FIGURE 4-11 Mary Lueck. *Woman With Flowers.* 1981. Pen and ink, 9″ × 12″. Courtesy the artist (student, University of Wisconsin—Milwaukee). In this stark and strict employment of bilateral symmetry, the head of the figure is centered to make it more conspicuous. The stasis is quietly challenged by irregularities in the flower shapes.

All these factors in photographic representation can vary much more than we realize. Of all the possible images that could be "objectively" recorded by exposing a sensitive surface to light, we take a minuscule percent—and most of those we throw away because they are unlike (or so we say) the nature of the thing represented.

Most people probably tend to think that the mere presence of a camera and film insures the production of a "realistic" picture. Others would depart from that belief, and some would even say that the relationship between a photograph and the thing represented is no more "realistic" than (as has been said of contemporary theories of physics) the relationship between a telephone number and the person whom we call.

The Relativity of Realism

The fallacy of Leonardo's rule might have been apparent to Leonardo himself if, at the time that he wrote it, he could have traveled to China. There he might have encountered artists who would have recommended rules identical to his own—but with quite different results.

In the ninth century, for example, the Chinese critic Chang Yen-Yuan complained about the lack of "realism" in Chinese art. "Few artists," Chang lamented, "can paint a fly looking so real as to be mistaken for a real one, and we see only those who end up by painting a tiger like a dog."

Chang and Leonardo appear to be saying the same thing. Both are asking that artists construct works of art which are most like the thing represented. However, if you asked each man to produce a "realistic" drawing of a table, the results would be strikingly dissimilar.

Leonardo would draw a tabletop in which the rear edge (the edge most distant from us) would be observably less wide than the edge which is in front. He would do this because he believed in *linear perspective*, the practice of symbolizing an increase of distance by a decrease in size. He would also paint in shadows of things (though not as much as we would today).

The apparent decrease in the size of things as their distance increases is known as *optical diminution*. The Chinese were aware of this concept, but they rarely used it. Accordingly, if you asked Chinese artists (contemporary with Leonardo) to draw a "realistic" table, they would most likely draw one in which the rear edge of the tabletop would be the very same width as that of the front edge. This is customarily referred to as *isometric perspective*.

PERSPECTIVE Any method by which a three-dimensional space is represented on a flat surface. Linear, aerial (or atmospheric), isometric, cabinet, and reverse perspective are most commonly used.

LINEAR PERSPECTIVE A system of perspective which was first popularly applied in fifteenth-century Italy. In this method, a progressive decrease in size is intended to depict a progressive increase in the distance of objects from a static viewing point.

OVERLAPPING The concealment of parts of one object in favor of the complete rendering of another object with the intention to depict that the former is behind the other while both are in our line of sight.

AERIAL PERSPECTIVE A method of signifying distance, invented by Leonardo da Vinci, in which nearer objects are sharply rendered (in advancing colors) and those which are more distant are progressively indistinct (in receding colors). It is virtually the same as atmospheric perspective, in which increasingly distant things are obscured by zones of mist.

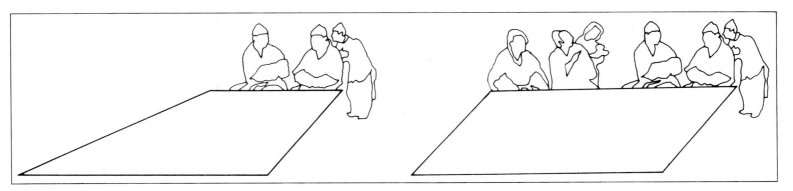

FIGURE 4-12 As indicated by these diagrams of tabletops, there is a remarkable difference between European linear perspective (on the left) and Oriental isometric perspective (on the right), even though both were attempts to make "realistic" pictures.

Why would Chinese draw this way? Probably because they believed that optical diminution was not a "real" attribute of tabletops (which, in fact, it isn't), and thus it was illusory. Tables do not *really* shrink as we walk away from them. It may be for the same reason that Chinese artists rarely painted shadows, since shadows are effects of light, not "real" characteristics of things. Whatever the reason, it certainly would not be that the Chinese were primitive; in virtually everything they did, they were among the most advanced.

The philosopher Nelson Goodman (who has written about realism with a clarity and incisiveness that I can never hope to meet) has said that "realism is relative, determined by the system of representation standard for a given culture or person at a given time."

Within the aim of this book, it is not possible to examine the enormous number and variety of styles of realism which could very well result if a person were simply asked to make a drawing which is most like the thing represented. A number of cultures have used size to indicate the social importance of figures (servants always drawn as small, whether they are far or near). Others have resorted to split representation, simultaneous multiple views, reverse perspective, transparency, stacking, bird's-eye views, and so on.

Suffice it to say that the variations have been so enormous in number and in kind that only the smallest percentage of people who have ever lived on earth would agree with or even be able to read the mode of representation which we

ISOMETRIC PERSPECTIVE A method of representing three-dimensional space, usually associated with Far Eastern art, in which all features of a thing are rendered in a common scale. Thus, an increase of distance is not indicated by a decrease in the size of things. As a result, size might then instead be used to indicate the affective or social importance of things (as when servants are drawn small and their masters are drawn large, regardless of their distances).

STACKING A common alternative to overlapping, in which an object is depicted as being behind another object by placing the former above the latter.

REVERSE PERSPECTIVE A system of perspective which is the approximate inverse of linear perspective, in that the sizes of things increase as their distances increase. This type of representation offers more information (or, at least, a different kind) than does linear perspective, in that three sides of things are shown in addition to the top.

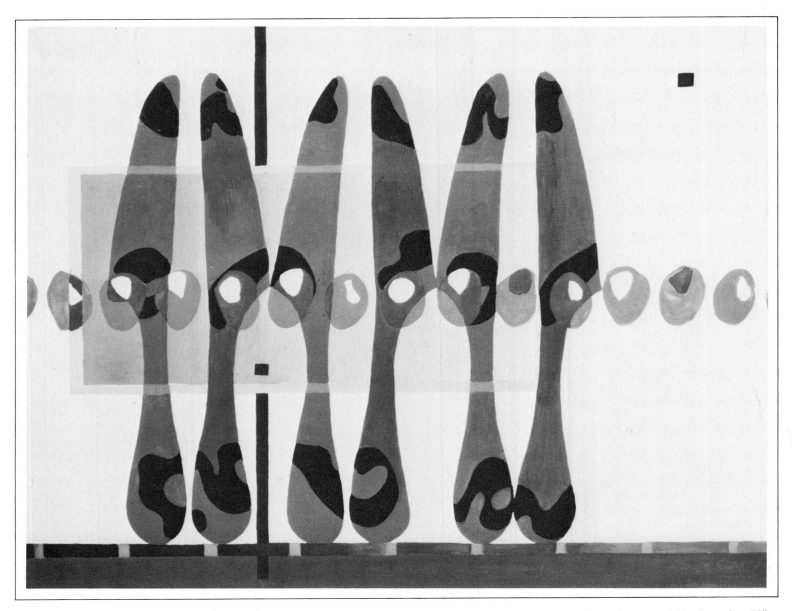

FIGURE 4-13 Catherine Ploetz. *Kitchen Knives, Bacon and Olives.* 1980. Gouache, 13″ × 17″. Courtesy the artist (student, University of Wisconsin—Milwaukee). This work was designed for a problem which specified a certain number of knives, olives, slices of bacon, and several rectangles. The predominant vertical and the large rectangle are shifted to the left. The knives are shifted to the right.

call "realistic." In fact, as I hope to have implied, probably *we* could not agree on what we mean.

The Child and the Artist

Small children, it is sometimes said, are like one-person cultures. Untrained in our traditions, they have no clear conception of the "proper" ways to see and draw. If you watch them when they draw, they often seem to rely on those "odd" ways of drawing things that have predominated in other cultures or our own culture at other times.

This range of styles is lost in school, perhaps because of teachers' ploys, but more because of pressure from their peers and parents to conform to the "realism" of adults.

Their loss of innocence is good (and unavoidable) in the sense that their adaptation is eased. It is unfortunate in that it restricts them—unless they are serious artists—to the narrower vision of *a single way to mean.* It is as if, when they were young, they spoke bits of German, Arabic, Swedish, and Navajo, but when they become adults, they speak only English—and a rather poor English at that.

When artists say (as some have and still do) that they hope to be like children, they have their tongue in cheek somewhat. They desire the flexibility and openness of a child—but with the wisdom of adults.

The most significant difference between children and adults is that adults who are wise realize the significance of their inventions. Children cannot do that, which is why they must be taught. They cannot know their works are new, because they do not know the old.

Children are creators because they are close to the mystery of their feelings. . . . Artists are gripped by the spontaneity with which children express themselves, making sovereign use of their paper and drawing implements and paying perspective and such things no heed.

Oskar Schlemmer, in *The Letters and Diaries of Oskar Schlemmer* Tut Schlemmer, ed. (Middletown, Conn.: Wesleyan University Press, 1972), p. 23.

Chapter 5

Vision and Invention

The Meaning of Metaphor

When I was an adolescent, I was told that a metaphor was a figure of speech or trope in which two things are compared without using *like* or *as*, for example, "my love is a rose."

This is perfectly true in a sense, but it did not let me know the enormous significance of metaphor. It was a decade later before I came to realize (after painful searching) that as Aristotle said, "The greatest thing by far is to be a master of metaphor." It is a sign of genius, he said, "since a good metaphor implies an intuitive perception of the similarity in dissimilars."

My strongest encounter with metaphor began when I was very young. There was a sewage ditch at the south edge of my parents' property. Around the ditch grew waist-high weeds.

Stalking slowly by the ditch, I would focus on the weeds, hoping to catch grasshoppers with my bare hands. Often when I did this, I would be peripherally aware of a tiny streak of brown or gray darting on the ground below. It was of

The invention of a metaphor full of illustrative power is the achievement of genius. It is to create by saying "no" to the old associations, the things that have constantly gone together, the things already sorted, and "yes" to new associations by crossing old sorts to make new ones.

Colin M. Turbayne, *The Myth of Metaphor* (Columbia: University of South Carolina Press, 1971), p. 57.

FIGURE 5-1 Richard Avedon. *Ezra Pound, Poet.* June 30, 1958, Rutherford, New Jersey, at the home of William Carlos Williams. Black and white photograph. Courtesy the artist.

On one of these Sunday excursions when I went along I remember that we amused ourselves during the long black blowy subway ride by playing the metaphor game: by turns each describing an inanimate object in such a way as to portray without naming a public figure. Jim developed a second-hand silver flute into Leslie Howard, and a Grand Rapids easy chair into Carl Sandburg.

Robert Fitzgerald (recalling James Agee) ed., *The Collected Short Prose of James Agee* (New York: Ballantine Books, 1970), p. 23.

course a field mouse. But it moved so quickly that no matter how quickly I switched my gaze, it would not be there when I looked. It was like looking at faint stars, which are distinctly visible when I look to the side of them but almost disappear when I stare at them directly. It was as if the field mouse was there and yet it was not there. It did not even move the grass.

This happened a number of times. It is a vivid memory of my childhood.

About six years after that, my attention was repeatedly drawn to a series of brief newspaper reports regarding the release from a mental institution of a man named Ezra Pound. Accompanying each article was a small photograph (always the same photograph) of, as the paper described him, this American poet who had been deemed a traitor during World War II.

I later learned of course that Ezra Pound had broadcast radio talks, in Italy, during the reign of the Fascists. He had been captured by the American army at the war's end, returned to Washington, and committed indefinitely to St. Elizabeth's mental institution.

Much later, I also learned that this Ezra Pound was one of the greatest poets of this century. But when I first took note of him, I only focused on his face (it was pained and gentle) and mused about his funny name, this man whose name was like a "pound."

Much, much later, when I was more than twenty-three, I found myself wandering aimlessly and depressed at night on an American naval station. Somehow, having finished college and having taught a year in high school, I had been drafted into the U.S. Marine Corps. With almost two years to serve, I thought of all the wishful things that I could be doing then—touring Europe or the United States, writing books like this one, teaching, or inventing things.

In desperation, while I walked, I went into the military library and looked for a book on the shelves (any book) that might give me some reprieve. To my surprise, I found a book by Ezra Pound, and when I broke the pages, I found these four lines:

And the days are not full enough
And the nights are not full enough
And life slips by like a field mouse
Not shaking the grass.

Here, within these lines, I found a way of thinking about the flight of time and my fear of never completing all those things I hoped to do. Of course, Pound's metaphor is "life is like a field mouse." It had great meaning for me because it brought together (within a single idea) two vivid memories of childhood (the

FIGURE 5-2 Nancy Wall. *Untitled.* 1978. Acrylic, 14″ × 18″. Courtesy the artist (student, University of Wisconsin—Milwaukee). In this exquisite visual pun, fish and egg are made to rhyme, and worms are rhymed with bacon.

FIGURE 5-3 K. Dyble Thompson. Brochure design for School of Fine Arts, University of Wisconsin—Milwaukee. 1979. Courtesy the artist. The legs of a camera tripod, this visual metaphor implies, are like the legs of certain birds.

field mouse and the face of Pound) and the frustration I felt. These seemingly different fragments now became a unit. It was then that I started to grasp the meaning and importance of making metaphors, whether in words or in visual forms.

Metaphorical Thinking

Before finding this poem by Pound, I had met another poet. He was an Iowa farmer and teacher named James Hearst, whose metaphors often spoke of certain features of farming as if they were other things.

Especially, I remember a poem called "Truth" in which he said that plowing a field was like searching for the truth in life. Are there "rocks" that one might hit? And the poem answers, "How the devil do I know if there are rocks in your field, plow it and find out," because as it later states, "the connection with a thing is the only truth I know of, so plow it."

The point of these examples is that I would like to show not just the function and significance of metaphors but also, more specifically, their function and significance in relation to visual esthetic design, the making of patterns and pictures. Artists constantly employ what is sometimes labeled *metaphorical thinking*. Accomplished artists, in terms of visual esthetic design, are excellent makers of metaphor, whether they know anything about poetry or not.

Now, what Pound said in his four-line poem can be said in other ways. In fact, we hear it every day, in commonplace expressions like "life is short" or "time sure flies" or "there just isn't time enough in the day." But these are neither poetic nor artistic expressions because, as one old saying goes, "It ain't *what* you do, it's *how* what you do it."

Poetic metaphor is a way of saying things, and what it says is usually not very new. In the same sense, a visual artwork is a way of conveying some feeling or thought, and what it conveys is usually not very new. Whistler was neither the first nor last to have a somber mother.

What Metaphors Do

When the word *metaphor* is used in a narrow way, it only refers to (as we said) a specific type of verbal trope which does not employ *like* or *as*. Used in that sense, it is distinguished from other figures of speech, such as similes, which are verbal

METAPHOR Narrowly defined, a trope or figure of speech in which a thing is spoken of as if it were the same as some other thing, which it is normally thought to differ from. Broadly defined, any action is metaphorical if a thing is treated as if it were some other thing, which it is usually thought to differ from.

How the devil do I know
if there are rocks in your field,
plow it and find out.
If the plow strikes something
harder than earth, the point
shatters at a sudden blow
and the tractor jerks sidewise
and dumps you off the seat—
because the spring hitch
isn't set to trip quickly enough
and it never is—probably
you hit a rock. That means
the glacier emptied his pocket
in your field as well as mine,
but the connection with a thing
is the only truth that I know of,
so plow it.

James Hearst, "Truth," from *Limited View* (Iowa City: Prairie Press, 1962).

METAPHORICAL THINKING Any style of thinking, perceiving, or behaving which is characterized by the intentional violation of habitual categories, resulting in unconventional sets. It is synonymous with *bisociation* (Arthur Koestler), *lateral thinking* (Edward de Bono), and *synectics* (William J. J. Gordon). It is creative thinking.

SIMILE A figure of speech which differs from metaphor in that a thing is spoken of as if it were *like* some other thing which it is usually thought to differ from.

comparisons in which *like* or *as* are used. Technically then, Pound was making a simile when he said that life is *like* a field mouse.

However, when *metaphor* is used in its broadest sense (and it is increasingly common to use it this way), it means any construction (verbal, visual, aural, and so on) in which an object (person, feeling, or event) is spoken of, represented, or in some way treated as if it were some other object (person, feeling, or event) which it is usually thought to differ from.

Thus, Hearst's statement is a metaphor for the very reason that "searching for the truth" is not the same thing as "plowing one's field." If they were the same thing, there would be no metaphor, or in some cases, a "dead metaphor," one that's used so often that the brand name has become generic (for example, "the *face* of the clock" or "the *legs* of the chair"). Anyway, the important point to make is that when metaphors are made, as when works of art are made, it is not only *likeness* which is essential but *difference* as well.

If a metaphor speaks of (or depicts or treats) one thing as if it were something else, to what extent must these two things differ? Some people have insisted, especially some surrealists, that the most powerful metaphors juxtapose two things which are vastly different or are even direct opposites, much like complementary hues.

This may or may not be the case, but it seems consistent with the principle of simultaneous contrast. As we saw in Chapter 2, the "redness" of the color red is most noticeably accentuated when it is placed on or next to the opposite color

---

The poet invents new juxtapositions of words and phrases which convey new thoughts. The inventor makes new juxtapositions of things which give new results. Neither the poet's word nor the inventor's things have any remarkable properties of their own. They are everyday words and things. It is the juxtaposition of them which is new.

David Pye, *The Nature of Design* (New York: Reinhold, 1964), p. 64.

DEAD METAPHOR   A metaphor which has been used so frequently that it has become a conventional phrase, for example, "the *mouth* of the river" or "*dead* metaphor."

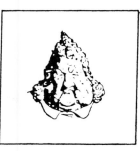
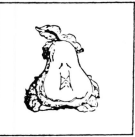

FIGURE 5-4   Charles Philipon. *Les Poires.* 1832. In this satirical drawing of King Louis Phillipe, two normally different things (king and pear) are treated as if they were one. Arthur Koestler has referred to creativity as a "marriage of cabbages and kings." This is a marriage of pears and kings.

of green. Perhaps in the same way, the concept of searching for truth may be accentuated (its "truthness" made more vivid) by being placed on or next to a concept as unlike as plowing one's field.

Creativity as Metaphor

In its widest definition, metaphor is sometimes said to be exactly the same process as creativity. To my knowledge, virtually all research and most theories of creativity support this notion, more or less. As a result, creativity need not be regarded as an elusive process which cannot be talked about. Providing our language is not impoverished, it can be discussed clearly, if it coincides with the widest definition of metaphor.

CREATIVITY   Broadly speaking, any kind of action (in any style or medium) in which one speaks of, represents, or in some way treats something (person, emotion, or event) as if it were some other thing, which it is usually thought to differ from. Unlike mistakes and madness, creative actions are characterized by a double awareness, in that the conventional grouping as well as the creative set are present in a single mind.

FIGURE 5-5   Robert Cumming. *Two Double Negatives.* 1974. Black and white photograph. Courtesy the artist. This photographer is often referred to as a "conceptual artist." However he might be labeled, he is at least a master of metaphorical seeing. Compare the two photographs. You will find in each two occurrences of the word *no.*

I do know that the whole of fantasy, poetry, ballet, and art in general owes its meaning and importance to the relationship which I refer to when I say that the swan figure is a "sort of" swan—or a "pretend" swan.

Gregory Bateson, *Steps to an Ecology of Mind* (New York: Ballantine Books, 1972), p. 34.

In other words, when we are creative (when we invent something new), *we speak of or in some way treat one thing (person, emotion, or event) as if it were some other thing, which it is usually thought to differ from.*

In this definition, the words *as if* are of the utmost importance, since they are meant to indicate that inventive or creative acts only pretend to confuse two different things. Pound was perfectly aware of the fact that life is not a field mouse. Hearst knew perfectly well that searching for the truth is not really (or literally) the same as plowing one's field.

This point is terribly vital, because it indicates the difference between those situations in which a person is creative and quite different situations in which a person is insane, childishly naive, mistaken, or outside the context of one's native culture. On the surface, actions of this latter kind often look like creativity, which sometimes encourages people (who do not understand this definition) to believe that artists are like children, or even that they are insane. In fact, creativity is, if anything, the antithesis of childlike naiveté or the mental confusion of madness.

The Stereoscope of Ideas

A man named William B. Stanford said that metaphor is a "stereoscope of ideas." Stanford was making a metaphor, since metaphors are not really stereoscopes. But we can better comprehend the way that metaphors (and creativity) operate by looking at the way that three-dimensional (3-D) pictures operate.

The essential factor of stereoscopic representation is *binocular disparity*, the fact that the eyes are separated. Hold an upright pencil at arm's length and alternately view it with one eye at a time—the right, the left, the right, and so on. The pencil will appear to move because the eyes are spaced apart, so that in normal vision, the eyes receive *two differing views* which the brain makes into one.

When 3-D photographs are made, the subject is simultaneously photographed by two cameras (side by side, as if they were two eyes) or one containing two lenses. When the pair of photographs are viewed one at a time, or both are viewed with both eyes, they appear to be as flat as any other photographs. But, when they are seen through a 3-D viewer (a stereoscope), the figure "pops out" from the background. Why? Precisely because the stereoscope replicates normal vision: It is designed in such a way that only one photograph is seen by the right eye and only the other photograph is seen by the left eye.

In a sense, metaphors are expressions which have remarkable depth or dimension. They are not flat statements as are most common expressions. Fur-

Art is always about turning two into three or three into two.

Paul Feeley, quoted in E. C. Goossen, *Ellsworth Kelly* (New York: Museum of Modern Art, 1973), p. 57.

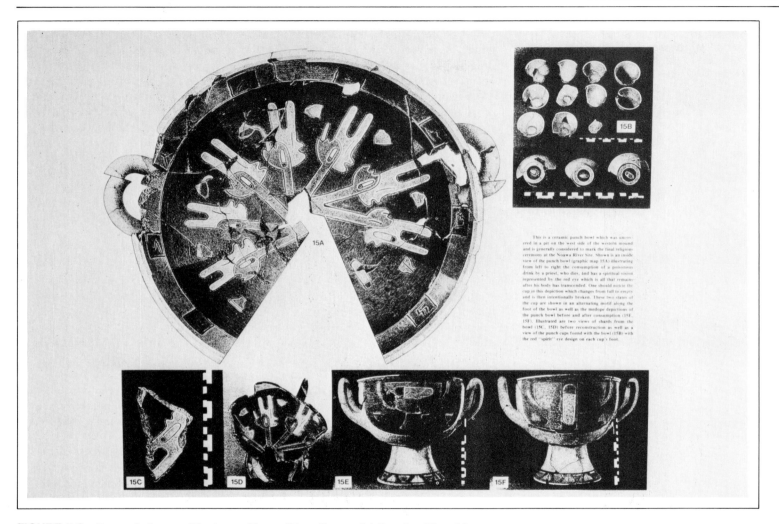

FIGURE 5-6   Beauvais Lyons. *The Arenot Noawa River Ceremonial Complex, Plate 15.*
1980. Lithographic print. Private collection. Courtesy the artist. This is one of fifteen
plates from a fictional archaeological show, which pretends to document the beliefs and
ceremonial practices of the Arenot people. The total installation includes museum
cases containing twelve clay vessels (built by the artist, then cracked and
reconstructed). Doctor Lyons refers to his work as "mock-archaeology."

ther, stereoscopes are like metaphors in several other curious ways. Both, it could be said, result in a fusion of differing things. In stereoscopes, the differing pair of pictures fuse. In metaphors, one thing (searching for the truth) is for a moment "con-fused" with something quite distinct from it (plowing one's field).

In metaphors and in stereoscopes, the two differing things must be viewed at the same time while still maintaining their separate characteristics. Thus, in stereoscopes, a 3-D illusion will not result if the two photographs are identical. In metaphors, if the one thing is the same as or too similar to the other thing, the result is either a weak metaphor or no metaphor at all (for example, "plowing one's field is furrowing one's field").

Finally, it might generally be said that metaphors and stereoscopes both involve paradoxical structures, the integration of diversities, or as Aristotle said, the "perception of the similarity in dissimilars."

Association and Bisociation

All the really good ideas I ever had came to me while I was milking a cow.
Grant Wood.

All this is much more complex than I am making it sound, and perhaps no one has better explained the nature of creativity than Arthur Koestler (in eight hundred pages) in *The Act of Creation.*

In that book, Koestler referred to creative thinking (or acting or seeing) as *bisociation,* to distinguish it from intelligent grouping, or normal *association.*

In intelligent acts (association), we group things together on the basis of certain similar features (remember the Gestalt unit-forming factors). For example, we say that elephants and mice are the same kind of thing (despite their differences) because they have in common certain essential features which are characteristic of things we call *mammals.*

In creative acts (bisociation), we group things together which are normally thought to be distinct on the basis of features which are usually ignored, since they are not essential. For example, one might say that elephants and Volkswagens are the same kind of thing because both have trunks up front.

In the same sense, Koestler would say that Pound was bisociating when he said that the passage of life is the same kind of thing as the passage of a field mouse, since "both are gone before you know."

Or he would say that Hearst was bisociating when he said that searching for the truth is the same kind of thing as plowing one's field, since "there are rocks and weeds in both" (and, sometimes, buried treasure).

music
performance

FIGURE 5-7 K. Dyble Thompson. Brochure design for School of Fine Arts, University of Wisconsin—Milwaukee. 1979. Courtesy the artist. There is, as Arthur Koestler says, a visual bisociation between the bowlike bill of the bird and the bill-like bow of the violin.

FIGURE 5-8 John Biersach. *Stop.* 1979. Mixed media construction, 30″ × 36″ × 3″. Courtesy the artist. Surprising insight can result when normally mundane objects (which one would usually ignore) are treated as if they were art. This artist builds and isolates simulated sections of walls from common architectural sites.

Much of Koestler's book is a documentation of how this same process works when a scientist invents something. For example, he traces the invention of the printing press by Johann Gutenberg (whose name at birth was *Gensfleisch,* meaning "gooseflesh"), who hoped to print the Bible.

To accomplish that task by fifteenth-century printing methods was virtually impossible. The printer would have had to carve each page of the Bible on woodcut blocks (backwards) and print it by rubbing the paper with a burnisher. In his correspondence, Gutenberg remembered how he considered other stamps and imprint devices (a punch for casting coins, the imprint of seals in wax, molds for making pewter cups), until he eventually thought of carving each letter as a separate piece of movable type, which could be assembled to print a page then reassembled for the next.

Yet so long as the rubbing method of printing remained, the process was too slow. An answer came to Gutenberg while he was drinking alcohol, so that his associative thinking had become somewhat relaxed. "I took part in the wine harvest," he recalled; "I watched the wine flowing, and going back from effect to cause, I studied the power of this press which nothing can resist. . . ." *Eureka!* He suddenly arrived at what he called a "simple substitution." It was a bisociation or metaphor. He thought, for only a moment, that *grapes* and *pieces of type* are the same kind of thing. He completed an analogy is which grapes-are-to-a-wine-press as type-is-to-a-printing-press. He went home and designed a printing press, which resembled and worked like the press in which the grapes were squeezed.

It is also reported that Eli Whitney, who was attempting to invent a device for harvesting cotton, was taking a walk when he saw two cats fighting through a wire fence. Neither could pull the other through, but each could grab a paw of fur. Whitney had an *insight* (the Gestaltists' term for creativity), which resulted in the cotton gin. It is essentially a machine containing a wire fence and mechanical fingers which pull the cotton seeds through the fence and leave the cotton on the other side. The bisociation is, of course, that cotton is the same as fur.

The Logic of Humor

If the examples of Gutenberg and Whitney are at all amusing, it may be (as Koestler showed) that humor is a subcategory of creativity. All jokes, puns, and witty remarks are based on pretended "con-fusions" of two or more distinctive things.

If lawyers are disbarred and clergymen defrocked, doesn't it follow that electricians can be delighted; musicians denoted; cowboys deranged; models deposed; tree surgeons debarked and dry cleaners depressed?

Virginia Ostman.

Punning . . . is an extremely important feature of all forms of symbolic communication but especially perhaps in areas of social life which are the focus of taboo such as sex and religion.

Edmund Leach, *Culture and Communication* (Cambridge, England: Cambridge University Press, 1976), p. 18.

In the films of the Marx Brothers, for example, Chico pretends to have an Italian accent which causes him to make "mistakes." When Groucho directs him to a viaduct, Chico responds with "Why a duck? Why ah no chicken?" Or when told of a wire fence (recall Eli Whitney), Chico asks, "Why a fence?" In discussing a written contract, Groucho suggests a sanity clause, to which Chico replies, "Ah, you no fool me. There ain't no Sanity Claus."

In the same way, Groucho substitutes "tusks are looser" for "Tuskaloosa," "irrelephant" for "irrelevant," and "I shot an elephant [which was] in my pajamas" for "I shot an elephant [while I was] in my pajamas."

It should be obvious by now that humorous designs depend (as do metaphors) on the simultaneous perception of two distinctive things which resemble each other in normally nonessential ways. Thus, our focus is suddenly switched

FIGURE 5-9 Robert Cumming. *Academic Shading Exercise.* 1974. Black and white photograph. Courtesy the artist. In the photograph on the left, the chalkboard drawing is negative and the surrounding "reality" is positive. In the photograph on the right (a negative print of the first), the chalkboard drawing is positive and the surrounding world is negative.

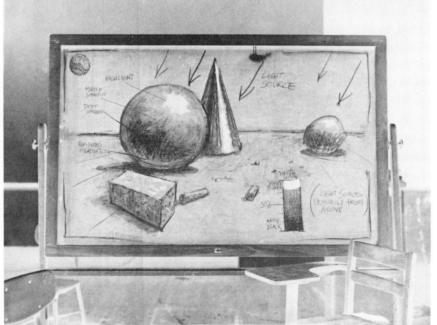

(in the punch line) to those "irrelephant" features so that a unit is formed which is logical in terms of comical thinking and irreverent in terms of routine daily thought.

Humor is also a stereoscope. One eye is the humorist; the other is the straight man. Thus, Don Quixote is twisted, and Sancho Panza is straight. Sherlock Holmes goes off on bents, whereas Doctor Watson stays on course. In most jokes, there is no need for straight men, since the audience is straight—they have routine thoughts in mind.

Creative Taxonomy

Whenever some new object or thought is created, two things occur: (1) It is shown that there is a surprising *similarity* among two or more things which were previously thought to be different. This is sometimes said to be "making the strange familiar." It is unit-making. And (2) it is shown that there is a surprising *difference* between two or more things that are normally thought to be similar. This is sometimes said to be "making the familiar strange." It is unit-breaking.

Carolus Linnaeus, the most important figure in the history of classification, said that things will be known to that person "who can join the similar to the similar, and can separate the dissimilar from the dissimilar." Linnaeus' scheme was absolute (God had opened "His cupboard" to him, Linnaeus said, and shown him the proper arrangement of things), but it was novel in its time, as when he contended that bats are not the same as birds, and whales are not the same as fish. In a sense, all inventions are modifications in taxonomy, or changes in classification.

It is not surprising then that a considerable number of jokes are based on taxonomic twists—as when Henny Youngman says, "Did you hear that they crossed a gorilla with a mink? They got a nice coat but the sleeves are too long." Or, "I heard they crossed a rooster with another rooster. The result was a very cross rooster." These are not so distant from a kind of comic Gutenberg, who crossed grapes with movable type to produce a printing press.

Creativity and Madness

Most people are surprised to find that creativity is exceedingly difficult. They think that if you "have it," it must be effortless to work.

It is difficult to invent (to be creative) primarily because we are usually rewarded (and, in that sense, conditioned) to pay attention to those grouping

Wit lies in the likeness of things that are different, and in the difference of things that are alike.
Madame de Staël.

Angels can fly because they take themselves lightly.
G. K. Chesterton.

FIGURE 5-10 Frank G. Lutz. *Cedar Series III*. 1980. Mixed media construction, 24″ × 38″ × 12″. Courtesy the artist. This work has certain features of esoteric devices of high technology, and yet it has no function other than esthetic. The spacing of each of its features has intentionally been designed to comply with the "golden section" or the "divine proportion," an ancient mathematical system.

FIGURE 5-11 K. Dyble Thompson. Brochure design for School of Fine Arts, University of Wisconsin—Milwaukee. 1979. Courtesy the artist. Two major puns are evident here. The open human hands on the left side are subtly reminiscent of the adult monkey's open palm, pressed against the floor. In the upper portion, there is a surprising resemblance between the monkey's curled tail and the stark white paper roll which is in the child's hands.

features which are normally emphasized and to ignore those grouping features which are normally ignored because (as grown-up tradition deems) they are irrelevant or nonessential. Throughout every day, we are repeatedly rewarded for acting in expected ways and not infrequently punished for acting in surprising ways.

When we do creative things (making jokes or metaphors), we only pretend, as we said before, to confuse two kinds of things. In fact, if we would go through life actually believing that searching for the truth is really the same thing as plowing one's field, we would find it hard to live. There are human beings who actually believe such things, and if we do not perceive their pain, they might at first appear to be telling jokes or inventing metaphors. These are people with severe emotional disorders or mental illnesses. They are usually characterized by disorders of association, which is to say they tend to group (to sort or categorize) in ways that most would see as odd.

The mad cannot knowingly invent. They cannot think routinely, so they cannot comprehend that a field mouse and one's life are not the same thing. The person who is mad, as Foucault has said, "takes things for what they are not, and people for another; he cuts his friends and recognizes complete strangers; he thinks he is unmasking when, in fact, he is putting on a mask . . . he is unaware of difference." The person who is mad is a stereoscope in which one eye is blinded. The artist is only pretending.

The Value of Creativity

What is the relationship between creativity and visual esthetic design? To put it all too simply, creativity *modifies* things, or (recalling Chapter 2), it enables the artist to make two different things appear to be similar (making the strange familiar) and to make two similar things appear to be different (making the familiar strange).

Invention is the best device by which we can avoid or change the anesthetic conditions of extreme similarity (humdrum) and extreme difference (hodgepodge), and by that arrive at the esthetic condition of unity with variety, in our art and in our lives.

Inventive modification, laced with logical thinking, is the most effective means by which we can design our lives—of which the ingredients may consist of poetry, games, cups of coffee, music, pocket calculators, jokes, bank robberies, firecrackers, or of course, the visual arts.

Indeed, William Blake was probably "cracked"—but that is how the light came in.
Dame Edith Sitwell.

Only art, *by the evocative use of language or by the vision of the painter which transcends the conceptual confines of language, can express more of what man experiences in his sensory contact with the world than the limitations of ordinary speech permit.*
Ernest G. Schachtel, *Metamorphosis* (New York: Basic Books, 1959), p. 165.

Part Two

Problems and Process

Chapter 6

Two-Dimensional Problems

Problem One

Holsteins are large dairy cattle with irregular patches of black on a white body. They were imported from Holstein, a formerly Danish dukedom which is now part of West Germany.

Holsteins are remarkably similar to certain examples of World War I dazzle camouflage. Against a pure white background, they tend to look like a random array of black patches rather than a single form. They also look like Dalmatian dogs, the mascots of firefighters. Holsteins and Dalmatians are like walking figure and ground diagrams. If the Gestalt psychologists had raised animals, I suspect they would have raised Holsteins and Dalmatians. They also would have wondered why we see these animals' coats as black patches on a white background. Why don't we see them as white patches on a black background?

The Gestalt psychologists found that circles are the simplest shapes. Every part of a circular shape directs us to a central point. There are no corners in circles, no sudden directional changes. Circles rivet the attention. Circles within circles or concentric circles are even more compelling. They are focal targets. Targets are carefully used in art because unbroken concentric circles can produce a static composition in which the target "steals the show" (distracts the viewer's eye) from other aspects of the work. The whole of the work is then ignored in favor of a single part.

For the opposite reason, checkerboard patterns are also used with caution. Chessboards and checkered tablecloths tend to have no focal point. They are the same all over, with no intriguing ups and downs, no surprising ins and outs. They are neither inspiring nor offensive. They are as unobtrusive as wallpaper or the piped-in music in office waiting rooms.

Checkerboard patterns become much more lively if the board is tipped in space, or as checkered cloths might do, if the pattern drops off an unexpected edge or flows around a nonsquare shape beneath it. Checkered patterns can also be disrupted by having colored squares in some irregular order, rather than the standard alternations of white and red or red and black. Or perhaps the board is cut, the cloth is ripped or folded, and so on.

Finally, let us consider a glazed and salted biscuit, which loops around and ties a knot. It is of course a pretzel, the name of which derives from the Latin term for "armlike cakes." For this problem, it is essential to look closely at a pretzel, not simply as a thing to chew but as a unique visual form, which is both like and unlike a host of other things in life.

The primary task of this problem is to develop a two-dimensional visual esthetic design. That is the most important requirement and, whatever else the students do, that should be foremost in their minds at all times. If their solutions are anesthetic—if the resulting arrangement is too monotonous or too chaotic—they have not solved the problem.

In addition, the work must incorporate the following clues:

1. The solution consists solely of black and white and various values of nonhue gray, obtained by mixing black with white. There are no hues in the work.
2. The work contains all or any parts of three concentric circles. These "targets" are of equal size, and each is comprised of at least four circles within circles.
3. The solution contains all or any parts of one checkerboard pattern which is surprising in some way(s). It might, for example, be tipped in space. It may be cut, ripped, or folded. Perhaps it is part of a cube. It might appear transparent. Perhaps it is a sheet or shroud in which some kind of shape is wrapped. It might disappear at times to reappear at other points, and so on.
4. The solution contains all or any parts of at least eleven pretzel shapes. These could be eleven repetitions of the same pretzel. If they are different pretzels, they are of the same general size. These can be depicted in any style, and they need not be shown as obvious "pictures" of pretzels.
5. The solution contains all or any parts of at least four patches from a Holstein cow. These could be four repetitions of the same patch. If they are different patches, they are of the same general size. They need not be black.
6. Any shapes may overlap. Any shapes may be cropped by the edges of the work. Any shapes may be partially hidden. Any shapes may be broken or fragmented by some other means. Any shapes may be combined with other shapes to make less recognizable shapes. Shapes may seem transparent or may be broken by changes in value.

Problem Two

In its narrow definition, the term *physiognomy* refers to the common practice of judging the inner characteristics of people (their personalities) by examining their outer characteristics—by reading the lines on their palms or feeling the bumps on their heads.

Several hundred years ago, it was commonly believed that the moles on people's bodies were analogically related to the stars and planets, and that people's fortunes could be reliably foretold by examining their moles. One of these systems predicted that if you had a mole on the back of the neck, you would die by hanging.

Giambattista della Porta, an eccentric Renaissance writer, claimed to have discovered that people can be classified by their physical and emotional resemblances to certain animals and plants. There are certain people, Porta said, who look and act a lot like pigs. There are other human types who are basically sheepish, bullish, catlike, birdlike, and so on.

In caricature and cartooning, famous people are often shown as if they were types of animals, for example, hawks and doves. When we intend to insult people, we often call them animal names—like turkey, chicken, snake, and weasel. It is also intriguing that a considerable number of our mythological and comic book characters are amalgamations of human and animal characteristics, such as Batman, the Green Hornet, Donald Duck, Dracula, and King Kong.

The primary task in this problem is to attempt to develop a two-dimensional visual esthetic design. Whatever else is done, the work must have an esthetic arrangement.

In addition, the work must incorporate the following clues:

1. The answer is based on a monochromatic color scheme. The students are, in other words, limited to the use of a single hue—any hue. They may use any number of different values or intensities of that particular hue. They may use black and white and any number of values of nonhue gray.

2. The work contains all or any parts of two repetitions of any geometric shape (squares, rectangles, pentagons, hexagons, and so on) which can be of any size.

3. The solution contains at least eleven pinstripes. They can be positioned horizontally, vertically, or diagonally. They might all follow the same direction, or perhaps they intersect or follow contrasting directions.

4. The work contains all or any parts of at least four repetitions of the face or figure of a famous person. This figure must be directly derived from a photographic source, by tracing, Xeroxing, or some other accurate copying scheme. These figures can vary in size.

5. The work contains at least one occurrence of all or any part of any thing or object which is not a human being, and which, in some surprising way, has a visual resemblance to that famous figure.

6. The solution contains any number of repetitions of any word. The meaning of the word may or may not have anything to do with the famous person.

7. Any shapes may overlap. Any shapes may be cropped by the edges of the work. Any shapes may be partially hidden. Any shapes may be broken or fragmented by any means. Any shapes may be combined with other shapes to make them more intriguing. Shapes may seem transparent. Shapes may be broken by changes in hue, value, or intensity.

Problem Three

The American painter Otto Harp was born in Montana in 1907, the year that Picasso completed *Les Demoiselles d'Avignon* (the first Cubist painting) and the Boy Scout movement was founded. He died (aged 51) in 1958, the year the stereo phonograph was invented.

This artist received widespread public attention in the early 1940s when it was revealed that he was married, at the same time, to three prominent operatic sopranos—Bertha Venation, Carmen Gia, and the notorious Eva Destruction.

Harp was among the most prolific artists of his time, since he completed a major work approximately every ten days. With only one exception, all his works have been located. Within the past few years, critics and historians have engaged in endless debates regarding the appearance (and disappearance) of this long-lost work of Otto Harp.

This mysterious painting seems to have been finished in 1932, the year that Franklin D. Roosevelt was first elected president and Shirley Temple appeared in her first motion picture (entitled *Red-Haired Alibi*). The painting vanished the following year.

The original work was viewed by only three persons other than the artist. From their descriptions, we know that the work was ahead of its time. It did not appear to be a painting from the 1930s. It is said that were we to see it today, it would appear to have been made within the past ten days.

The problem is to reconstruct the long-lost work of Otto Harp (who, of course, never existed). Those who saw the painting have supplied the following clues:

1. It was a superb example of visual esthetic design.

2. It was a rectangular two-dimensional work.

3. It has been described as having an analogous range of predominant hues, with direct or indirect complementary accents. Most of its hues were modified—their values were evidently high or low, and their intensities had been lowered to some degree.

4. It contained at least two occurrences of reversible figure and ground.

5. It included all or any parts of at least three shapes which had been derived from neckties. One of these was a polka dot pattern (in whole or part), and the other two had stripes.

6. It contained at least ten shapes which had been derived from the pieces of any kind of breakfast cereal.

7. It also contained all or any parts of at least four shapes which had been derived from high-heeled shoes.

8. Some shapes may have overlapped. Some may have been cropped by the edges of the work. Some shapes may have been partially hidden. Some shapes may have been broken or fragmented. Some shapes may have been combined with other shapes. Some shapes may have been transparent. Some shapes may have been interrupted by changes in hue, value, and intensity.

Problem Four

Some of the conditions of this problem will be determined by chance, by playing a common children's game, which is sometimes called "Consequences" or "Boggles." I have also heard it called "Grandpa Splashed Happily in the Bathtub." The game is usually played with words, but a pictorial variation was used by the dada and surrealist artists as a way of making art. They called it "The Exquisite Corpse."

To begin the problem, each student is given a blank sheet of paper. On cue, all participants simultaneously write down the name of any person or thing (for example, *Grandpa*) which first comes to mind. The paper is then folded so that the name cannot be seen and is passed on to someone else. Then, again on cue, each person writes a verb (*splashed*), folds the paper and passes it on. This same procedure continues, the paper being passed each time, until an adverb (*happily*), a preposition (*in*), and a noun (*the bathtub*) have been selected. At the end, the papers are passed a final time. Each paper is then unfolded to reveal a more or less meaningful sentence, for example, "Clark Kent applauded bluely into the sewing machine," or "The typewriter sang shyly on top of the orange juice."

Obviously, no two persons will end up with the same sentence. Some sentences will be humorous, some will be strange, and some may be perfectly reasonable. Each sentence will serve as the title of the work to be designed by the person who received it. The basic shapes of which the work will be comprised are to be developed from the visual characteristics of the persons or things which are listed in each sentence.

As in the previous problems, the primary goal is to develop a two-dimensional visual esthetic design. In addition to that requirement, and the use of any number of all or any parts of the items contained in the title, it must incorporate the following clues:

1. The color scheme within the work consists of a triadic range of predominant hues. Virtually all occurrences of these hues have been modified by alterations of value and intensity.

2. The work contains at least three examples of a cognitive contour.

3. The work is based on an underlying grid system, which consists primarily of horizontal and vertical axes, with diagonal axes as accents.

4. As before, any shapes may overlap. Any shapes may be cropped by the edges of the work. Any shapes may be partially hidden. Any shapes may be broken or fragmented. Any shapes may be combined with other shapes to make them more intriguing. Shapes may seem transparent. Shapes may be interrupted by changes in value, intensity, and hue.

Problem Five

To begin this problem, each student must randomly select any novel which he or she has never read. Without looking at the text, the student must quickly open the book to any page of text.

The problem is to develop a two-dimensional visual esthetic design in which at least some of the shapes in the work are derived in part or whole from the contents of that page of the novel. The work may or may not illustrate (that is, describe or be a picture of) the scene or action on the page.

In addition, the work must incorporate the following clues:

1. The predominant hues in the work are based on a split-complementary scheme. In other words, there are three predominant hues. Two of those hues are indirect complements (to the left and right of the complementary hue) of the third. Most occurrences of the hues have been modified in intensity or value so that even though the colors are remarkably different as hues, they are similar in value and intensity. Black, white, and gray, as well as additional hues, may also occur in smaller amounts.

2. There are areas in the work, large or small, which remind one of corduroy fabric.

3. There are areas in the work, large or small, which invoke certain textures, surface patterns, or other general features that might be found on house plants.

4. There are at least two examples of coincident disruptive patterns contained in the work.

5. As in all previous problems, any kind and number of shape modifications are encouraged. Any shapes may overlap. Any shapes may be cropped by the edges of the work. Any shapes may be partially hidden. Any shapes may be broken or fragmented. Any shapes may be combined with other shapes. Shapes may seem transparent. Shapes may be disrupted by changes in hue, value, and intensity.

Problem Six

The completion of this problem requires that each student obtain two actual postage stamps from a hobby shop, post office, or stamp exhibition. The stamps can be from any country. They can be antique or current, franked or unfranked. They might be two copies of the same stamp or two entirely different stamps. They should be selected for the quality of their design, their use of color (which may or may not include hues), and their pictorial richness.

The final work will be horizontal in orientation. It will measure about 9½″ by 4¼″, the dimensions of a business-size envelope.

The problem is to devise a two-dimensional visual esthetic design which, in one way or another, incorporates two postage stamps. In addition, the following clues apply:

1. The work is polychromatic, but the color scheme is not specified for this problem since it will have to be chosen with the colors of the stamps in mind.

2. Somewhere in the work, in large or small amounts, there is at least one occurrence of a line or shape or texture which one would refer to as "zigzag."

3. The work must *not* comply with normal postal regulations for the placement of stamps, and so on. Other than its size, it need not bear any similarity to a usual envelope.

4. Included in the work are at least three examples of a broken continuity line.

5. In addition to these clues, any number of other devices might also occur. Perhaps they are derived from the visual characteristics of the stamps; perhaps not. Any shapes (including the stamps) might be partially hidden, fragmented, cropped, overlapped, broken, disrupted, combined, and so on.

Problem Seven

In preparation for this problem, the instructor will need to select two works of art, each by a different artist. The works might be historical, contemporary, or both. It would be best if they were excellent examples of visual esthetic design. The problem is especially rich if the two works are radically different in style. They might also be different in subject matter, technique, use of color, and so on.

Slides or other reproductions of the two works are presented to the class, and the students (with the guidance of the instructor) thoroughly examine each work, making a list of its visible features (especially its compositional traits). It may help, in doing this, to pretend that one is describing the works to a person who is blind.

Having arrived at two separate lists of characteristics (one list for each artwork), the problem is to develop a two-dimensional visual esthetic design which incorporates some of the characteristics of the works which were analyzed. For example, the general kind of color scheme (analogous, triadic) might be derived from one of the works, whereas the actual hues might be borrowed from the other; or certain shapes

could be adopted from one, and another set of shapes derived from the other; and so on.

If the two initial works are sufficiently different and complex, there will be no shortage of distinctive features to choose to use or not. It is important to emphasize that the final result of this problem may have little if any *obvious* resemblance to the two initial works.

Finally, as always, any shapes may be partially hidden, fragmented, cropped, overlapped, broken, disrupted, combined, transparent, and so on.

Problem Eight

In presenting this problem, the teacher must bring to the class three intriguing objects of any sort—decorative articles, exotic vegetables, kitchen utensils, and so on. These are in a box or bag. They are never shown to the students, and their identities are never revealed.

While looking at these objects (which the students cannot see), the teacher makes a verbal list of twelve visible attributes which are characteristic of one or more of these objects. This list is recorded by the students, and the items are numbered from one to twelve.

The problem is to develop a two-dimensional visual esthetic design which is like the secret objects in terms of all even-numbered attributes but which is unlike those objects in terms of all odd-numbered characteristics. Accordingly, if feature number 6 is *square*, the final work must incorporate a square. And if feature number 9 is *green*, the final work will use instead a hue which is distinct from green, such as red or orange; and so on, throughout all the attributes.

Any variety of compositional features may be used in addition to these. And as in the previous problems, any shapes may be partially hidden, fragmented, cropped, overlapped, broken, disrupted, combined, transparent, and so on.

Problem Nine

This problem is partially determined by the students in that they are free to choose from a lengthy list of clues. It is also determined by the instructor in that the list of clues consists of all those which have been included in all the previous problems. It is unlikely that any two students will select identical sets of clues, so that every student will be dealing with a more or less different problem.

The problem is to devise a two-dimensional visual esthetic design which incorporates at least six clues, each from a different problem. For example, one might select the Holstein patches from Problem One, the pinstripes from Problem Two, the color scheme from Problem Three, and so on, until at least six clues are used.

Any variety of compositional features may be employed in addition to these. And as is always specified, any shapes may be partially hidden, fragmented, cropped, overlapped, broken, disrupted, combined, transparent, and so on.

Problem Ten

Each student is asked to devise a problem which is intended to produce a two-dimensional visual esthetic design. The problems are submitted in a clearly written form. The papers are shuffled and redistributed, so that each student is assigned a problem of which he or she is not the author.

Chapter 7

Three-Dimensional Problems

Problem One

To *gamble* is to play a *game*. Both words come from *gamen*, Old English for "amusement." In order to amuse themselves, hunters go in search of "game." If I want to be amused, I might say that "I am game." In one form or another, games occur throughout the world.

This problem is concerned with games with boards and pieces. They sometimes come in boxes. Think of the board as a playing field or *ground*. Think of the pieces as *figures*, so that when the game is viewed, it looks like a painting that changes.

The students are asked to develop the gameboard, box, and pieces for a game for which the rules are lost. They imagine, for example, that they have been transported to some exotic culture from the past, present, or future. They do not understand the language and customs of this culture. Suddenly they find a box (or similar container) in which a

board and parts are housed. The box is either unlabeled or labeled with indecipherable words. They wonder what this object is—and yet they have an inkling, simply from the way it looks, that this must be some kind of game.

The solution to this problem might be entirely three-dimensional, or it might also be partially two-dimensional. The board and the box might be separate objects, or the box might somehow also be the board. The board, box, and pieces might be built entirely by hand. Or it might be more intriguing to alter objects which you find in toy stores, hobby shops, doll-house furniture stores, junk shops, and hardware stores.

The primary goal of this problem is to develop an assemblage or construction in which the board, box, and pieces appear to belong together, in terms of visual esthetic design, because of their visual attributes. The solution should also be inventive. The vast majority of commercial games and gameboards are designed with very little regard for esthetics or visual inventiveness. As a result, they tend to be symmetrical, simplistically colored, generally poorly composed.

In addition, the work must incorporate the following clues:

1. The predominant hues are based on an analogous range of hues with split-complementary accents. Throughout the work, most occurrences of the hues have been modified in intensity or value.

2. There are certain objects, areas, or aspects of the work which bear some resemblance to one or more characteristics of peas within a peapod.

3. The work contains any number of objects, shapes, or aspects which *vaguely* look like hockey sticks.

4. The students are encouraged to experiment with any kind and number of modifications. Any objects, shapes, or spaces may be broken or fragmented. Any elements may be combined with other elements. Any parts may be partially hidden. Parts may be transparent or only seem transparent. Any objects, shapes, or spaces may be interrupted by changes in hue, value, and intensity.

Problem Two

Albrecht Dürer, the sixteenth-century German painter, once observed that if one wants to picture dreams, one should "freely mix all sorts of creatures," fusing random parts of things into one strange hybrid form, somewhat like a dragon.

Nearly half the sleeping time of newborn infants is occupied by dreaming. Adults tend to dream one and one-half to two hours during each eight-hour period of sleep. People prevented from dreaming tend to feel a loss of coordination and general irritability.

The content of dreams is often expressed in visual images and somatic rumblings of one sort or another, with little if any reliance on words. For this and other reasons, Arthur

B. Fallico has said that "if we seek for an object which resembles the art-object, we will find none better than the dream."

During the eighteenth and nineteenth centuries, dreams were often considered to be absurd and meaningless. It was an invention of Freud to contend that dreams make sense. The dream as we recall it, he said, is its *manifest* content, which is a logically camouflaged form of its *latent* meaning. Because that meaning is disguised, repressed subconscious motives do not interrupt our sleep.

Freud emphasized three major strategies by which the mind disguises dreams: (1) *symbolization* (or substitution) in which one thing stands for or takes the normal place of some other thing, based on some kind of resemblance; (2) *condensation* (which is what Dürer talked about), in which parts of two or more things are recombined to form a mysterious hybrid thing; and (3) *displacement,* which works by a switch of attention, in which our focus is misled (much like the use of decoys in military and natural camouflage) so that we are distracted from the most important parts.

This problem has to do with the logic that occurs in dreams. If the problem had a name, it might be entitled "The Mind at 4:00 A.M.," which is an intentional parody of the title of a sculpture by the Swiss sculptor and painter Alberto Giacommetti, who in 1933 made a dreamlike room entitled *The Palace at 4:00 A.M.* It is commonly reproduced in books about surrealist art, but to avoid preconceptions of how this problem might be solved, it might be advisable not to look it up until the problem has been solved. In general, this problem tries to show the mind as if it were an open room in which a dream is taking place.

First, and foremost, the answer must result of course in a three-dimensional work which is a visual esthetic design. In addition, the following clues must be incorporated:

1. There are no hues in this design, and accordingly, there are no changes in intensity. The students are restricted to the use of white, black, any values of nonhue gray, or

any combination of the three. They are, as well, encouraged to experiment with value changes which result from shadows.

2. In general, the solution will consist of a miniature three-dimensional roomlike space which can be viewed from all four sides as well as from the top. It would be wise for the students to remember that they are not being asked to make a "model" of the brain. Instead, they are depicting a roomlike space in which a dream is taking place.

3. In one way or another, most or all of the shapes in this work appear to contradict our commonsense understandings of normal reality. In most of our daily encounters, for example, we assume that one thing cannot be in two places at the same time, that two things cannot occupy the same space at the same time, that objects are affected by gravity, that objects appear smaller to the eye as their distance increases, and so on. Other violations of normal reality might best be developed by studying the three methods by which dream forms are disguised—symbolization, condensation, and displacement.

4. Within the solution, there are all or any parts of at least three repetitions of shapes which *vaguely* bring to mind sections of a hacksaw, potato chips, and halos.

5. Again, students are encouraged to invent any kind and number of modifications and surprises. Any objects, shapes, or spaces may be broken or fragmented. Any elements may be combined with other elements. Any parts may be partially hidden. Any objects, shapes, or spaces may be interrupted by changes in value.

Problem Three

Reuben Lucius Goldberg was born in San Francisco in 1883 (the year that Robert Louis Stevenson wrote *Treasure Island*); he then moved to New York where he became one of the most popular syndicated cartoonists of the twentieth-century. He called himself Rube Goldberg.

Rube Goldberg became famous for his cartoon drawings of "Professor Butts," an absent-minded academic who contrived absurd contraptions requiring numerous steps to accomplish simple tasks.

In one of his cartoons, for example, a man pulls his tooth in the following way: He ties himself to a chair, then wiggles his foot, which tickles a duck. The laughing duck shakes an alcoholic drink tied to its back, then falls forward, spilling the cocktail on a squirrel in a revolving circular cage. The cocktail makes the squirrel drunk, which turns the cage, which turns the crank on a phonograph, which plays a record. The music enrages a dwarf, who gets "hot under the collar." Flames from the dwarf's hot collar ignite a fuse which causes a cannon to fire. The cannonball is attached to a string, and the string is attached to the tooth of the man. At last, the man has pulled his tooth.

The primary task of this problem is to develop a three-dimensional visual esthetic design. That is the most important requirement and, whatever else the students do, that should remain foremost in their minds at all times. If the solutions are anesthetic—if the resulting arrangement is too monotonous or too chaotic—they have not solved the problem.

In addition, the work must incorporate the following clues:

1. It is characterized by a triadic color scheme. Most of the hues in the work have been modified in value or intensity.

2. The student is to devise and build an operating three-dimensional mechanism which could best be titled a "Rube Goldberg Drawing Machine." It can employ any kind of automation (rubber bands, water, steam, small animals, air, spring mechanisms, motors, and so on) as long as, once it is started, it can operate itself. In the process of operating, it must make some kind of mark

(lines, drips, splashes, smudges, or whatever) on any kind of surface, to qualify as a "drawing" machine.

3. The problem is not restricted to purely visual media. The answer might also make use of sound, movement, smell, and so on.

4. The solution can be developed within any style. It may be built entirely by hand or by recombining available mechanisms and other "found objects." It does not have to resemble the original cartoons of Rube Goldberg.

Problem Four

As discussed in Chapters 1 and 3, there are two major kinds of camouflage. In *blending* camouflage, an object is so similar to its background that it is no longer visible as a separate thing. In *dazzle* camouflage, a perplexing variety of highly differing shapes are applied to the surface of the object so that it is hard to see as a cohesive, single thing. These two approaches are often combined, so that parts of a dazzle scheme might also blend in with the background.

The essence of this problem is the development of a three-dimensional visual esthetic design in which a combination of blending and dazzle camouflage schemes have been used to obscure or to complicate the outlines of various objects which have been mounted on a base. In addition, the following specifications apply:

1. The color scheme is polychromatic. It might also use unmixed black and white as well as nonhue grays.

2. The work contains at least three occurrences of coincidental disruptive patterns.

3. The solution contains at least two examples of a broken continuity line.

4. The work includes any number of false shadows—shapes which appear to be caused by light but which, in fact, are painted value changes.

5. Finally, as always, any parts may be fragmented, cropped, partially hidden, overlapped, broken, disrupted, recombined, and so on.

Problem Five

In preparation for this problem, each student is asked to provide as many identical objects or shapes as there are persons in the class. These pieces are distributed, so that every student is given one of each of the items. Thus, if there are fifteen people in the class, each student will end up with fifteen different objects or shapes, and every member of the class will have the same collection.

The problem is to recombine these randomly chosen objects or shapes in such a way that they belong together as a three-dimensional visual esthetic design. Because of their diversity, most or all of the parts may require considerable modification through surface alteration, cropping, partial concealment, overlapping, disruption, recombination, and so on.

The color scheme might also be selected randomly, by assigning number values to various hues and then tossing sets of dice; by blindly selecting three numbers, then finding the colors which match them in a color notation manual such as the Pantone Color Specifier (Designer's Edition of the Pantone Matching System); or less randomly, by choosing any three hues which appear on a package or label.

Problem Six

This problem requires the invention and construction of what could be called a "self-portrait toy." However, it asks for neither the usual portrait nor a conventional toy.

To initiate the problem, it is necessary for each student to think about his or her own customary manner of speaking, moving, and thinking. What style of structural features (elements of design or grouping attributes) is most like that person? What kinds of color schemes are most appropriate, for example, blatant or subtle distinctions of hue, high difference or low difference combinations? What values and intensities are most characteristic? Should the hues be warm or cool? If there were characteristic shapes, would they be curvilinear (expressing gradual changes) or angular, soft or sharp, large or small? Is the personality fuzzy or clearly defined? Are the major axes vertical, horizontal, or diagonal? In determining these attributes, it may be helpful for the students simply to look in their own clothes closets, since most people tend to buy styles, colors, and textures of clothing which in some way "look like" them.

Having determined the most appropriate hues, values, intensities, textures, shapes, and so on, the students are to use these features in the development of a three-dimensional visual esthetic design which is, in some inventive way, a kind of nonpictorial toy.

Problem Seven

This is a three-dimensional variation on two-dimensional Problem Four, listed in Chapter 6. The problem is begun in exactly the same way, so that each student is assigned a more or less meaningful sentence, which serves as the title of the work. The basic shapes within the work are to be developed from the visual characteristics of the persons or things which are listed in the sentence.

The primary goal of the problem is the development of a three-dimensional visual esthetic design. In addition to the use of any or all parts of the items contained in the title, it must incorporate the following clues:

1. The color scheme within the work consists of a direct complementary range of predominant hues. Virtually all occurrences of these hues have been modified by alterations of value and intensity.

2. The work contains any number of shapes which look like parts of venetian blinds.

3. There are at least two shapes or spaces in the work which invoke barber poles.

4. There is a surprising use of at least two small mirrors in the work.

5. As in all previous problems, any number and kind of alterations might occur, including partial concealment, overlapping, transparency, shape disruption, and so on.

Problem Eight

This is a combination of two-dimensional Problems Seven and Eight, described in Chapter 6. In preparation, the instructor must select two three-dimensional works of art, each by a different artist, historical or contemporary. They should be prime examples of visual esthetic design, but they should radically differ in the styles or kinds of features used.

While examining the works, the students (with the guidance of the instructor) make two parallel lists of at least ten features of the works. The items are correspondingly numbered in each list, 1 through 10. Thus, item 1 in both lists would note the kind of hue scheme which each particular work employs. Item 2 might note the color intensity of the works, and so on.

The problem is to develop a three-dimensional visual esthetic design which is like the characteristics of one of the works in all even-numbered attributes and like the characteristics of the other work in all odd-numbered attributes. The final result of the problem may have little if any obvious resemblance to the two initial works.

Problem Nine

As in two-dimensional Problem Nine, this problem is partially determined by the students in that they are free to choose from a list of specifications which have been included in all previous three-dimensional problems.

The problem is to devise a three-dimensional visual esthetic design which uses at least six clues, each from a previous three-dimensional problem. Thus, one might select peas within a peapod from Problem One, a roomlike space from Problem Two, hacksaw shapes from Problem Two, a triadic color scheme from Problem 3, and so on, until six clues have been chosen.

Any variety of compositional features may be used in addition to these. And as always specified, any features may be inventively recombined, fragmented, made transparent, overlapped, disrupted, and so on.

Problem Ten

Each student is asked to devise a problem which is intended to produce a three-dimensional visual esthetic design. Each student then completes the problem which he or she has written.

Appendix

On Teaching Design

It is a pleasant irony that one learns more from teaching than one learns from being taught. My ideas have evolved, as have my pedagogic ploys. I could not have written this book ten years ago. Nor is it the book that I hope to write ten years in the future. It is an *approximate* statement which must be viewed with some reserve, since if there are basic truths, Clive Bell may have offered three: "that what we believe is not necessarily true; that what we like is not necessarily good; and that all questions are open."

This particular part of the book is addressed to teachers of visual esthetic design, but students are welcome to eavesdrop, especially since, as some have said, *the ultimate goal of teaching is to assist one's students in learning how to teach themselves.*

This book was developed from courses in "foundations" which I have repeatedly taught at the University of Wisconsin—Milwaukee since 1976. Those in the basic course are almost entirely first-year students who are untrained in visual

arts, and surely in visual esthetic design. The vast majority intend to specialize in fields outside of art, from business administration to nursing. Thus, the first few weeks of class consist of a series of introductory talks on the theory of design, on how design relates to life, on what the course is all about. It is from those lectures that I developed the first part of this book.

Throughout each semester, I show my students the works of professional artists from the past and present. I also show them students' works which have resulted from the course. The latter is helpful, I find, because it gives them some clear sense of the level I expect. I choose and talk about these works in terms of visual esthetic design.

When selecting works to show, I make a conscious effort to present a wide range of styles, from highly detailed "realist" works (the paintings of Richard Estes, for example) to those which do not "picture" things (for example, constructivist art). At a risk I choose to take, I do not restrict their works to geometric abstract forms, as some textbooks might suggest, since visual esthetic design can be found within any kind of art, whatever the style or medium used. Further, as I have tried to show, the line between "patterns" and "pictures" is not as clear as one might like.

I tend to specify techniques, not because I teach techniques, but in fact because I don't. I may require a single medium throughout much or all of the semester (especially in the basic course), so that technique is not a stumbling block to the more important task—that of learning to design. In terms of visual esthetic design, the chief importance of technical skills is that they enable the viewer (including the artist) to distinguish similarities from differences, repetitions from variations. There is a necessity then for some degree of accuracy and consistency, but both of these can be achieved throughout the range of styles of art, from the most spontaneous modes to the planned and preconceived.

When I teach drawing courses, I teach drawing. When I teach design courses, I do not teach drawing. I do not require my students to draw, because we have a limited time and drawing can only be mastered through hours of disciplined practice. It may require more or less the same number of hours to learn to play the violin, so that in the same sense, if I were teaching musical composition to beginning students, I would not hand them violins—I would probably use kazoos, pocket combs, and empty jugs.

Further, when students use their self-drawn shapes, the drawings take such time and care that the students are reluctant to change them, to rearrange or recombine. The act of repositioning forms, manipulation and recombination, is the essence of design. As a result, I encourage the students to trace, to copy with projectors, to use ready-made techniques, or to use any mechanical aids for innovative shapes which can then be recombined.

My particular courses are scheduled to meet two days each week for a period of three hours each day. Each semester is fifteen to eighteen weeks in length. I assign eight to ten major studio problems within each semester. The students are given a specified time (usually ten days) from the day the problem is given until the finished work is due. The problems become increasingly vague as the semester progresses, until in the final problem, I may ask the students to both *assign* and *solve* a work.

The date on which the problem is due is an inflexible deadline. The deadline is part of the problem, and works which are submitted late do not receive full credit.

On days that finished works are due, the next problem is presented and assigned. This is followed by a lengthy critique in which each completed work is examined in the class. Each work is praised (for its strengths) and criticized (for its weaknesses). The major portions of the critiques are used to discuss all the works in terms of *visual esthetic design*. Additional factors are also discussed, especially aspects of technique (the accuracy and consistency of the medium employed) and presentation (the matte or base which "frames" the work).

All critiques are conducted anonymously. I do not know who made the works. During the critiques, the students do not reveal which works are theirs. Our comments are restricted to a directed review of the visible merits of the works, with the same anonymity with which they might be publicly shown. Regardless of its author, the work must stand on its merits.

Through anonymous critiques, I am better able to separate the personalities of students from their actual works. I am not trained in psychology, and it is not my business to judge my students' personal traits. It is my responsibility to criticize their art. As fair as one might try to be, biases are pervasive. I have repeatedly watched myself, when I knew who was the artist, tend to be more critical of works by students I dislike, and (just as damaging) less candid, too forgiving, of those by students whom I like.

This method does one other thing, which may be its greatest advantage. It prevents the student from thinking that failings cited in the work are not within the work at all but in my biased attitude toward his or her personality. By anonymous critiques, personality factors (as vital as they are in other contexts) are virtually dispensed with, and almost all our efforts are redirected toward the work.

I am able to conduct anonymous critiques because no works are completed in the classroom. When I first began the course, I chose to work outside of class because of inadequate studio space within the classroom and because it would require that students carry with them a considerable load of tools and materials, which is simply impractical. In addition, there were two other paramount factors.

First, it seemed to me (recalling my days as a student) that the atmosphere of working in class is the exact opposite of the surroundings one should have in working on a problem. I asked myself how I would feel if I had to work in class. I work best when I'm alone, with hot cups of chicken broth, background music, and my repertoire of tools. I require intense concentration, which can hardly be maintained with people at my elbows, engaging in casual chatter.

Second, a major part of what I teach is linked with self-reliance. Students should be exposed to at least a simulation of the uncertainties, loneliness, and utter frustration which all artists undergo. *Students should not be taught to rely on teachers. They should be taught to rely on themselves.* I do not coach them step by step. Aside from setting up the game and cheering from the sidelines, I coach them at each finished stage.

For some of the reasons I've stated, students are not permitted to discuss a specific solution with me until after its critique. However, while working on a problem, they may consult (in fact, they are encouraged to) any available sources or persons other than myself. Further, I will answer general questions at any time, as long as the questions they pose do not reveal their works to me. This is a "problem" in itself, which can be solved in clever ways, such as enlisting another student to ask a specific question or asking the question in a form that is disguised.

It is important to emphasize that once the work has been criticized, I will respond to any and all questions regarding it or I will criticize it at length with an individual student. Much of our scheduled classroom time is used for individual critiques and conferences.

Any work can be revised or completely remade at any time until the semester concludes, at which time all works are due.

It may seem incongruent that throughout each semester, I continually emphasize what might best be thought of as a kind of cursory "scavenger hunt" (some would call it *brainstorming*). I think few would disagree that both creativity and visual esthetic design are most apt to be brought about by the manipulation and recombination of things or shapes which are at hand, or at least within our reach. As Henri Poincaré once remarked, "fortune favors the prepared mind," and we might best prepare the mind not only by leaving it open but also by intensively stuffing it with a virtual potpourri of seemingly disparate concepts, off-hand observations, spurious speculations, and (especially in art) an encyclopedic range of styles and kinds of visible things, whether they are art or not.

Anything is grist for art, since anything and everything can be displaced and rearranged. Ways of promoting this scavenger hunt range from guiding my students to especially rich library sources (*The American Thesaurus of Slang*, the journals of *Leonardo*, or *The Encyclopedia of World Art*), to peculiar anecdotes, to intriguing classroom guests, to brief presentations on anything that is sufficiently odd (sometimes art and sometimes not) to probably be recalled, whether now or ten years hence.

When I first adopted this method, it had partially occurred to me by recalling my years as a student. Throughout the time I spent in school (from kindergarten through graduate school), my most vivid memories are not of truths that teachers preached but (as Zeigarnik's law predicts) of puzzles that they posed or of odd unplanned events which, at that time, did not fit.

This seemingly purposeless browsing is in contradiction to the blatantly specified part of the course in which a traditional value is taught, the value of visual esthetic design. I want that contrast to occur, since "gaps" are as vital to learning as are neatly packaged "facts."

The proper function of a teacher is neither to withhold all clues (in which the student provides everything) nor to allocate whole truths (in which the student has nothing to do, short of so much busywork). Teaching lies between the two, if (as Liam Hudson said) a truly effective instructor "must transmit an intellectual tradition with gusto, and instill a loyalty to it, but leave open the possibility of gradual or even revolutionary change." Teachers are makers of problems. They must not usurp the role of filling gaps between the clues, since that is how the student learns.

In Chapters 6 and 7, I have listed twenty classroom problems in visual esthetic design. These problems are purposely open and closed. They resemble riddles. They consist of lists of clues, and it is then the students' task to build esthetic structures which incorporate these clues.

There is no single answer to any of these problems. Unlike conventional puzzles, there are as many answers as there are persons who solve it. Or each problem can be solved repeatedly by the same person. In fact, if artists are inventive, they can repeatedly address the same problem throughout the entirety of their lives, and yet each work they make is new.

Obviously, when problems such as these are used, except in a very approximate way, no one can anticipate how the problem will be solved. The only way to solve the task is to take the leaps and risks which each student has to face.

Depending on the level of the students, it is important to avoid problems which are excessively open (especially early in the semester) and which are excessively closed (especially late in the semester). Problems which have no restraints do not give sufficient clues. Problems which are tightly closed do not immerse the students in the arduous visual juggling act which the course might hope to teach.

On rare occasion, I may employ an "exercise," but, despite the peripheral values they have, rudimentary exercises in texture rubbing, color mixing, value gradation, and so on are simply isolated parts. The whole is not the sum of parts, and no amount of "warm-up tasks" can even begin to replicate the greater problem-solving act, which is what I intend to teach.

The first ten problems listed here are designated as two-dimensional, the second as three-dimensional. I have divided the problems into those two categories because it is a widespread practice in college and university programs to offer separate courses in two-dimensional and three-dimensional design.

However, the two-dimensional problems need only be slightly altered to be used as three-dimensional problems, and vice versa. Were I to design a more suitable curriculum, I would probably not maintain the separation between the two categories, since as recent artworks demonstrate, it is increasingly difficult to distinguish readily two-dimensional works of art from those which are three-dimensional. Paintings have become increasingly sculptural, and sculptures have become increasingly painterly.

The merits of two-dimensional versus three-dimensional forms of art have been debated at least since the Renaissance, but I have yet to be convinced, in terms of visual esthetic design, that the principles and sensibilities used in two-dimensional design are of significant difference from those in three-dimensional works. There are differences of technique and material obviously, but those can be adapted to, and three-dimensional design is probably somewhat more difficult, since artists are dealing with multiple views and nonillusory depth in space.

The problems listed here are representative of a type of problem I have successfully (judging by the students' works) assigned to first-year, sophomore, and upper level students since I began to teach design. They are, as you will notice, repetitions of *the same problem*, simply garbed in varying robes.

In some cases, they are actual problems which in fact have been assigned while this book was being written. In other cases, they are simply prototypes, which I may or may not use.

My own philosophy is such that I prefer never to use the same problem twice. So that I might become better at problem making (as well as to surprise myself), I make a determined attempt to invent new sets of problems each semester. That is not as difficult as it sounds, since there is, as I've implied, an underlying structure which characterizes every problem: *provide some clues and leave some gaps*. The only real difficulty in problem making is in trying to decide precisely which clues to include, how many to offer and how many to hide.

As mentioned previously, I include more clues at the beginning of the course, then fewer and fewer as time goes on so that the students are gradually weaned. As teachers will no doubt detect, I try to choose intriguing clues—the patches of a Holstein cow, pinstripes, targets, and so on—which I have purposely gathered by browsing through dictionaries, encyclopedias, antique shops, catalogs, kitchen drawers, and works of art. I search for shapes and patterns which might enchant the human eye and which are reasonably accessible to the students.

These problems are not "teacher-free." Neither are they "teacher-proof." Whether they succeed or not will in actual fact depend on the enthusiasm, sensitivity, and resourcefulness of the teacher who assigns them. The problems as I list them here are only part of the actual classroom presentation. If they are not accompanied by the common sense, intelligence, and playfulness of a skilled and sensitive teacher, probably none of them will work.

As I list the problems here, I do not mention a specific medium, and yet, I very often do in class. I do not specify a size, and yet I often state a size in the first three or four

problems in the course. In addition, I give brief demonstrations of the basic requirements of matting and mounting. And if I require a certain medium, I introduce the students to it. I may suggest brushes and papers to use and so on. Finally, as I've implied, these problems are preceded and accompanied by selected slides of works by students and professionals, which I repeatedly discuss in terms of visual esthetic design.

Those who have not taught this way may understandably believe that these problems are too difficult for beginning students. Indeed, they are difficult problems *because making art is hard*. That they are not too difficult, I offer students' work as proof. I would urge those teachers to try to use these problems, or at least similar problems which make use of clues and gaps.

My students are not children. They are intelligent adults who, however young they seem, have dealt or are expected to deal with much more complex tasks (for example, the problems of marriage or of raising a child) than those that I devise. I have been asked to teach them art, and art is no less difficult than those "more serious" pursuits like premedicine, engineering, and calculus. In fact, it may even be harder, precisely for the reason that all the clues are not prescribed.

Further, in a certain sense, the difficulty of these problems is not within the problems but in the possible answers. With remarkable success, Edward de Bono (in *The Dog Exercising Machine* and *Children Solve Problems*) has presented even more challenging problems to British school children, who ranged in age from five to twelve. Invent a device, de Bono asked, which will "stop a cat and dog fighting" or which can "weigh an elephant." Or "invent a sleep machine," a "bicycle for postmen," and so on. These problems are undoubtedly difficult for any age group—but any age group can respond.

An Annotated Bibliography

I am familiar with hundreds of books, journals, and other sources which, to one degree or another, deal with visual esthetic design. They range from superb to inane. In this bibliography, I have listed very few. It is a nonstandard and highly selective listing of works that I have found of value in learning and teaching about design.

Most of the following sources are readily available in college and university libraries. Many contain bibliographies by which further works are indicated.

General Sources

Encyclopedia of World Art. 15 vols. New York: McGraw-Hill, 1959. Highly reliable, comprehensive summaries of an enormous range of topics. Each article concludes with an extensive bibliography on the subject.

MURRAY, PETER, AND LINDA MURRAY. *A Dictionary of Art and Artists*. Middlesex, Eng.: Penguin Books, 1976. Short entries on styles, techniques, and artists.

OSBORNE, HAROLD, ED. *The Oxford Companion to Art*. Oxford, Eng.: Oxford University Press, 1970. Concise, clearly written encyclopedic guide to history, theory, and artists.

STROEBEL, LESLIE, HOLLIS TODD, AND RICHARD ZAKIA. *Visual Concepts for Photographers*. London and New York: Focal Press, 1980. Not for photographers only. An excellent handbook and illustrated glossary of art, perception, and design.

Art History

CONE, MICHELE. *The Roots and Routes of Art in the Twentieth Century.* New York: Horizon Press, 1975. Lucid accounts of major movements since 1900.

HOLT, ELIZABETH G. *A Documentary History of Art,* 3 vols. Garden City, N.Y.: Doubleday Anchor Books, 1957 (vol.1), 1958 (vol. 2), and 1966 (vol. 3).

RICHARDSON, JOHN ADKINS. *Modern Art and Scientific Thought.* Urbana: University of Illinois Press, 1971. Insightful account of modern art in relation to major scientific developments.

SYPHER, WYLIE. *Rococo to Cubism in Art and Literature.* New York: Vintage Books, 1960. Intriguing theory of coinciding stylistic developments in visual arts, literature, and other fields.

WINGLER, HANS. *Bauhaus.* Cambridge, Mass.: MIT Press, 1978. Huge collection of documents and photographs regarding this important school.

WITTKOWER, RUDOLF, AND MARGOT WITTKOWER. *Born Under Saturn: The Character and Conduct of Artists.* New York: W. W. Norton, 1969. The most engaging, delightful art history book I know of. Traces the origin and development of popular myths about artists, including art and madness, artists as debauchers, starving artists, and so on.

Artists on Art

GHISELIN, BREWSTER, ED. *The Creative Process.* Berkeley: University of California Press, 1952. A classic anthology of introspective essays by artists, writers, and others.

GOLDWATER, ROBERT, AND MARCO TREVES, EDS. *Artists on Art.* New York: Pantheon Books, 1945. Valuable collection of excerpts from diaries and other writings of artists from the fourteenth to the twentieth century.

HERBERT, ROBERT L., ED. *Modern Artists on Art.* Englewood Cliffs, N.J.: Prentice-Hall, 1964. Manifestoes and other writings by Kandinsky, Mondrian, Klee, and others.

LIBERMAN, ALEXANDER. *The Artist in His Studio.* New York: Viking Press, 1969. Summarized interviews with major European modern artists.

RISENHOOVER, MORRIS, AND ROBERT T. BLACKBURN. *Artists as Professors.* Urbana: University of Illinois Press, 1976. Candid conversations with musicians, painters, and sculptors who teach in universities.

RODMAN, SELDEN. *Conversations with Artists.* New York: Devin-Adair Company, 1957. Summarized interviews with American modern artists.

ROSNER, STANLEY, AND LAWRENCE E. ABT, EDS. *The Creative Experience.* New York: Dell Publishing, 1970. Interviews with prominent scientists, artists, and writers about how they work.

SCHLEMMER, TUT, ED. *The Letters and Diaries of Oskar Schlemmer.* Middletown, Conn.: Wesleyan University Press, 1972. Fascinating record of the thoughts and fears of a gifted Bauhaus artist.

Design Theory

ALBERS, JOSEF. *Interaction of Color.* New Haven, Conn.: Yale University Press, 1972. Discusses simultaneous contrast and related phenomena.

DONDIS, DONIS A. *A Primer of Visual Literacy.* Cambridge, Mass.: MIT Press, 1973. Extensive listing of unit-making versus unit-breaking strategies.

HARLAN, CALVIN. *Vision and Invention: A Course in Art Fundamentals.* Englewood Cliffs, N.J.: Prentice-Hall, 1970.

ITTEN, JOHANNES. *The Art of Color*. New York: Van Nostrand Reinhold, 1974. Written by the first director of the Bauhaus foundations course. Also see his *Design and Form: The Basic Course at the Bauhaus* (New York: Van Nostrand Reinhold, 1976).

KEPES, GYORGY. *Language of Vision*. Chicago: Paul Theobald, 1969. One of the first attempts to apply Gestalt theory to visual esthetic design.

LAUER, DAVID A. *Design Basics*. New York: Holt, Rinehart and Winston, 1979. Clearly organized review of traditional elements and principles of design.

MAIER, MANFRED. *Basic Principles of Design*, 4 vols. New York: Van Nostrand Reinhold, 1977.

WONG, WUCIUS. *Principles of Two-Dimensional Design*. New York: Van Nostrand Reinhold, 1972. Seems to be addressed to architects rather than artists, but the illustrations are stimulating. Also see his *Principles of Three-Dimensional Design* (New York: Van Nostrand Reinhold, 1977).

Art Theory and Esthetics

ALLAND, ALEXANDER, JR. *The Artistic Animal: An Inquiry into the Biological Roots of Art*. Garden City, N.Y.: Anchor Press/Doubleday, 1977. Good discussion of anthropological and biological aspects of esthetics.

BEHRENS, ROY R. *Art and Camouflage: Concealment and Deception in Nature, Art and War*. Cedar Falls: North American Review, University of Northern Iowa, 1981. History and theory of natural camouflage, military camouflage, cubism, Gestalt theory, and creativity, considered as figure and ground modulations.

CIARDI, JOHN. *How Does a Poem Mean?* Boston: Houghton Mifflin, 1959. Classic discussion of design in poetry, most of which is applicable to the visual arts.

GARDNER, HOWARD. *Artful Scribbles: The Significance of Children's Drawings*. New York: Basic Books, 1980. Recent fresh explanation of how and why children draw as they do.

LEACH, EDMUND. *Culture and Communication*. Cambridge, Eng.: Cambridge University Press, 1976. Dazzling introduction to the theories of Claude Lévi-Strauss and other structural anthropologists.

MEYER, LEONARD B. *Emotion and Meaning in Music*. Chicago: University of Chicago Press, 1956. Gestalt theory applied to musical composition.

MOHOLY-NAGY, L. *Vision in Motion*. Chicago: Paul Theobald, 1947. Wide-ranging views of art and human life by a prominent Bauhaus teacher.

OSBORNE, HAROLD. *Aesthetics and Art Theory*. New York: E. P. Dutton, 1970. Lucid overview of the history and theory of esthetics by an accomplished writer and theorist. Includes excellent bibliography.

PECKHAM, MORSE. *Man's Rage for Chaos: Biology, Behavior and the Arts*. New York: Schocken Books, 1967. Fascinating theory of art in relation to human survival.

VENTURI, LIONELLO. *History of Art Criticism*. New York: E. P. Dutton, 1964. Historical review of theories of art and esthetics.

WECHSLER, JUDITH, ED. *On Aesthetics in Science*. Cambridge, Mass.: MIT Press, 1981. Includes essays on structural hierarchies and broken symmetries in art and science.

Art, Perception, and Psychology

ARNHEIM, RUDOLF. *Art and Visual Perception: The New Version*. Berkeley: University of California Press, 1974. Famous overview of the elements and principles of design in relation to Gestalt theory. Also see his *Visual Thinking* (Berkeley: University of California Press, 1971).

COTT, HUGH B. *Adaptive Coloration in Animals.* London: Methuen, 1940. Still the best description of animal camouflage and mimicry, with exquisite illustrations by the author, a prominent zoologist and military camoufleur.

GOMBRICH, E. H. *Art and Illusion: A Study in the Psychology of Pictorial Representation.* New York: Pantheon Books, 1960. An important history and theory of picture-making. His more recent companion volume, a history and theory of patternmaking, is *The Sense of Order: A Study in the Psychology of Decorative Art* (Ithaca, N.Y.: Cornell University Press, 1979).

GOMBRICH, E. H., JULIAN HOCHBERG, AND MAX BLACK. *Art, Perception, and Reality.* Baltimore, Md.: Johns Hopkins University Press, 1972. Essays on art and perception by an art historian, psychologist, and philosopher, respectively.

GOODMAN, NELSON. *Languages of Art.* Indianapolis, Ind.: Bobbs-Merrill, 1968. A theory of representation by a highly respected philosopher.

GREGORY, R. L. *The Intelligent Eye.* New York: McGraw-Hill, 1970. Discussion of representation (including stereoscopic pictures) in relation to visual perception.

GREGORY, R. L., AND E. H. GOMBRICH, EDS. *Illusion in Nature and Art.* New York: Charles Scribner's Sons, 1973. Includes excellent essays on natural camouflage and mimicry and pictorial representation.

HENLE, MARY, ED. *Vision and Artifact.* New York: Springer Publishing, 1976. Essays assembled by an authority on Gestalt theory.

HOGG, JAMES, ED. *Psychology and the Visual Arts.* Middlesex, Eng.: Penguin Books, 1969.

KEPES, GYORGY. *The New Landscape in Art and Science.* Chicago: Paul Theobald, 1956. Famous comparison of modern art and scientific photographs by the author of *Language of Vision.*

LORAN, ERLE. *Cezanne's Composition.* Berkeley: University of California Press, 1943. Exhaustive analysis of design and distortion in Cezanne's works.

PIRENNE, M. H. *Optics, Painting and Photography.* Cambridge, Eng.: Cambridge University Press, 1970. Excellent comparison of photography and perspective.

PORTMAN, ADOLF. *Animal Forms and Patterns.* New York: Schocken Books, 1967. An analysis of natural design in wide variety of natural forms.

TEUBER, MARIANNE L. "Sources of Ambiguity in the Prints of Maurits C. Escher." *Scientific American,* July 1974. Intriguing review of reversible figure and ground and related phenomena.

ZAKIA, RICHARD. *Perception and Photography.* Rochester, N.Y.: Light Impressions Corporation, 1979. Not so much a book about photography as it is a simplified introduction to Gestalt theory which uses photographic examples. Also see his excellent *Perceptual Quotes for Photographers* (New York: Light Impressions Corporation, 1980).

ZUSNE, LEONARD. *Visual Perception of Form.* New York: Academic Press, 1970.

Creativity and Metaphor

ADAMS, JAMES. *Conceptual Blockbusting.* San Francisco: San Francisco Book Company, 1976. Excellent overview of problem solving and strategies for creative thinking.

BARNETT, H. G. *Innovation: The Basis of Cultural Change.* New York: McGraw-Hill, 1953. Fascinating anthropological account of creativity.

DAVENPORT, GUY. *The Geography of the Imagination.* San Francisco: North Point Press, 1981. Essays on writing and writers by a highly respected essayist, translator, and fiction writer.

DE BONO, EDWARD. *Lateral Thinking.* New York: Harper and

Row, 1970. For purposes of visual art, this may be the best of his numerous books on thinking in inventive ways.

FRY, WILLIAM F. *Sweet Madness: A Study of Humor.* Palo Alto, Calif.: Pacific Books, 1968. Humor considered in relation to paradox and double-bind theory.

GORDON, WILLIAM J. J. *Synectics: The Development of Creative Capacity.* New York: Collier Books, 1968. Excellent discussion of metaphorical thinking and how best to practice it.

JENCKS, CHARLES, AND NATHAN SILVER. *Adhocism: The Case for Improvisation.* New York: Doubleday, 1972. All about putting the right things together in the wrong way or putting the wrong things together in the right way.

KNELLER, GEORGE. *The Art and Science of Creativity.* New York: Holt, Rinehart and Winston, 1965. Solid summaries of major theories of creativity.

KOESTLER, ARTHUR. *The Act of Creation.* New York: Macmillan, 1964. To my knowledge, still the most thorough and ambitious account of creativity throughout all of human life. His numerous other books are also of significance.

PICKERING, GEORGE. *Creative Malady.* New York: Dell Publishing, 1974. Consideration of the possible correlation between periods of high creativity and psychoneurotic illnesses.

SHIBLES, WARREN. *Metaphor: An Annotated Bibliography and History.* Whitewater, Wisc.: Language Press, 1971. An essential sourcebook if one wants to be a master of metaphor. Also see his essay "The Metaphorical Method," *Journal of Aesthetic Education,* April 1974, pp. 24–36.

TURBAYNE, C. M. *The Myth of Metaphor.* Columbia: University of South Carolina Press, 1971. Insightful and elegant book about the difference between things and the representations of things and about treating the menu as if it were stew.

VERNON, P. E., ED. *Creativity.* Middlesex, Eng.: Penguin Books, 1970. An anthology of research.

WATZLAWICK, PAUL, JANET HELMICK BEAVIN, AND DON B. JACKSON. *Pragmatics of Human Communication: A Study of Interactional Patterns, Pathologies, and Paradoxes.* New York: W. W. Norton, 1967. Good review of paradox, ambiguity, and double-bind in relation to schizophrenia, humor, and creativity.

Problems and Exercises

DE BONO, EDWARD. *The Dog Exercising Machine.* New York: Simon and Schuster, 1970. A book of children's drawn solutions to a challenging problem. Nine more problems and lots of answers are offered in his *Children Solve Problems* (New York: Harper and Row, 1974).

ELFFERS, JOOST. *Tangram: The Ancient Chinese Shapes Game.* Middlesex, Eng.: Penguin Books, 1976. Hundreds of problems in "visual thinking"—thinking with things in front of the eyes rather than thinking inside of one's head.

KOCH, KENNETH. *Wishes, Lies, and Dreams: Teaching Children to Write Poetry.* New York: Vintage Books, 1971. Highly successful approach which could easily be applied in the visual arts.

LALIBERTE, NORMAN, AND RICHEY KEHL. *100 Ways to Have Fun with an Alligator and 100 Other Involving Art Projects.* Blauvelt, N.Y.: Art Education, Inc., 1969. A stimulating book of problems. More serious, but no less playful, than the title.

MCKIM, ROBERT. *Experiences in Visual Thinking.* Monterey, Calif.: Brooks/Cole Publishing Company, 1972. Excellent introduction to visual perception, with exercises.

RAUDSEPP, EUGENE. *Creative Growth Games.* New York: Harcourt Brace Jovanovich, 1977. Brief warm-up exercises in problem solving and inventive thinking.

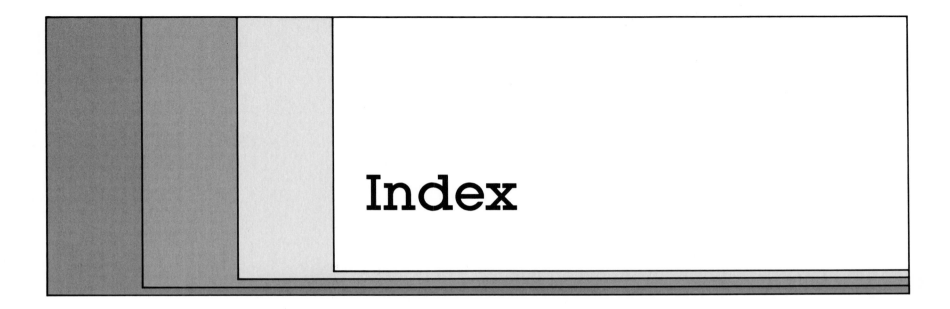

Index